Building Flexible Organizations:

A People-Centered Approach

Miles H. Overholt

KENDALL/HUNT PUBLISHING COMPANY
4050 Westmark Drive   Dubuque, Iowa 52002

ISBN 0-7872-1756-5

Printed in the United States of America
10 9 8 7 6 5 4 3 2 1

Contents

Preface   *v*

Introduction   *vii*

Section I
Building Flexible Organizations
1

Chapter One
Tools for Building Flexible Organizations   3

Chapter Two
People-Centered Organizations®   19

Chapter Three
Building Your Own Flexible Organization   41

Section II
Viewing an Inflexible and a Flexible Organization
57

Chapter Four
How Organizational Inflexibility Creates Dysfunction   59

Chapter Five
A Flexible Organization in Action   77

Section III
Changing Individuals and Teams in Flexible Organizations
95

Chapter Six
The Interplay Among Individuals, Teams, and Organizations   99

Chapter Seven
Shifting to Flexibility   109

Chapter Eight
Implications   131

Bibliography   135

Preface

I have three major obligations to fulfill in this preface: (1) stressing that the theoretical framework developed is not new theory, but a blend of theory and practice based on the great educators and practitioners; (2) thanking all the executives, managers, and employees who have educated me over the years; and (3) thanking my family and my colleagues at work for their unlimited support.

I developed the "People-Centered Organizations®" framework presented in the first section from my knowledge and understanding of the many brilliant theoreticians identified in the bibliography. I am fortunate in having been educated in two disciplines—organization and management theory, and family systems change and psychotherapy—and have used these disciplines as the base for building my approach to organizational change. My goal in writing this book is to present an approach to organizational change that blends these and other disciplines to make living through and managing transitions easier for all involved.

Perhaps the most exciting development in the nearly twenty years that I have been practicing is the increased intermingling of formerly separate and disparate disciplines. Today, developments in physics, archeology, biology, and traditional Chinese medicine significantly influence how organizational theorists, consultants, and management practitioners think and act. The multi-disciplinary age has truly arrived, greatly improving our ability to understand and influence organizations. This confluence of great theories and ideas serves to underscore my point; I simply have tried to integrate what I understand so that I can use it as skillfully as possible.

I have had the privilege of working with many people over the years in many different companies and industries. I am indebted to all of them for sharing their wisdom and knowledge, and for their patience with my learning. When I finsihed graduate school, I was fascinated by reading and studying how organizations worked, but had no real understanding of the dynamics of organizations until I had worked with hundreds of people. From all these people I learned that organizations are nothing but their people. I have worked with failing companies and incredibly successful companies, only to find that the people in each had the same dreams, hopes, fears, and capabilities. The major determinant between what made the bad companies bad and the good companies good was the degree to which they tapped their people's capabilities.

I need to express a special debt to my family. I added the extra hours required to write this book to an already too busy schedule. Both my wife and my daughter have always encouraged me and allowed me to slink off into another room to write when the mood struck. My wife, Debbi, has listened to the genesis of this book for many, many years, and never once tried to destroy my computer, an amazing act of self-restraint. My daughter, Becky, also gets a special thanks. We sat together on Saturday mornings, doing our homework, writing page after page, each wondering if we would ever get done.

I must include a special thank you to my partners and colleagues—Ted Connally, Kathy Crowley, Ken Prager, Sherri Merl, and Maureen Leer—who encouraged me to write and who spent hours discussing and reviewing the manuscript. I must recognize three of these colleagues for their invaluable contributions. I thank Kathy Crowley for her years and years of support in developing the perspective outlined in the book. Ted Connally's "alter ego" discussions and enthusiasm encouraged me to write the book. A special thank you to Ken Prager for editing. He was a major help in trying to make sense of this book, as was Swarna Mohan. I am also indebted to all those other colleagues with whom I have worked over the years and all of whom challenged me to make sense of organizational change.

Miles Overholt
July 30, 1995
Hilton Head Island

Introduction

"The shrewd guess, the fertile hypothesis, the courageous leap to a tentative conclusion—these are the most valuable coin of the thinker at work."

Jerome Seymour Bruner
The Process of Education

The need to build, manage, and lead flexible organizations that respond to rapid shifts in the marketplace has never been greater. The highly-competitive global economy of the 1980's and 1990's demands that organizations rapidly respond to market shifts or suffer the consequences. Well-known, market leaders such as GM and IBM, have suffered and lost their market leadership positions because they did not respond rapidly to changes in the market. Their executive teams were unable to foresee the upcoming market shifts, and to change their organizations to meet the needs of the market, once they were confronted with these shifts.

The age of pursuing a steady, well-proven strategy and building a stable organization to meet the needs of a clearly defined and stable market is gone. Executives are instead confronted with an era when they must anticipate rapid market shifts, develop new strategies, and redesign their entire organization to compete effectively. The highly competitive, rapidly changing global economy dictates that executives will need to become as capable of building and rebuilding organizations to meet specific market opportunities as they were of building traditional, stable organizations.

Consequently, executives, academics, and consultants are searching for the best way to build and manage flexible organizations. Not surprisingly, they have developed many different ways to build the organizations they need. Their proven results demonstrate that there is no definitive way to build and maintain flexible organizations. What is right for one company may be wrong for another. To determine what best suits them, executives need to use a design process that builds on their company's strengths and uniqueness. This process requires executives to:

1. understand their markets and determine strategies to succeed in them;
2. design the organizational structures and processes that can best deliver the strategy;
3. assess their current organizational structure and processes;
4. identify what needs to change from the current assessment to the ideal desired organization;
5. predict what will happen as they change the organization;
6. manage the change process as they implement the identified changes, and
7. repeat the process as markets change or new markets develop.

This book focuses on steps 2-7: designing, building, and maintaining flexible organizations. It is intended to assist executives and managers in identifying, developing, and maintaining the right way to build their flexible organization by:

1. introducing a framework, People-Centered Organizations®, to design and assess organizations;
2. discussing basic principles of how organizations function to predict and manage change;
3. illustrating the process of building flexible, People-Centered Organizations®; and
4. demonstrating how People-Centered Organizations® change occurs at individual, team, and organizational level.

Section One discusses these basic principles. Section Two presents case studies illustrating the key points. Section Three develops more depth to the basic principles, showing how individual change is strongly connected to and similar to organizational and team change.

The premise is simple. Organizations are living, dynamic entities, populated by humans. Humans are complex creatures that respond and adapt, in predictable and unpredictable ways, to external environmental pressures. Organizations are full of these external pressures—policies and procedures, salaries, and peer expectations. The best way for executives to lead their organization's people in a common direction is to have as many as possible of the organizational pressures guide people in the same direction, reducing unpredictable responses and adaptations. To accomplish this, executives need to learn how to create an organization congruent with the company's purpose and strategy. The congruency creates organizational influences and pressures that guide all employees to achieve the organization's goals.

Section I
Building Flexible Organizations

"I repeat . . . that all power is a trust; that we are accountable for its exercise; that, from the people, and for the people, all springs, and all must exist."

Benjamin Disraeli

"Man is a tool using animal . . .
Without tools he is nothing, with tools he is all."

Thomas Carlyle

"It is a test of true theories not only to account for but to predict phenomena."

William Whewell

Chapter One
Tools for Building Flexible Organizations

"Absolute continuity of motion is not comprehensible to the human mind. Laws of motion of any kind become comprehensible to man only when he examines arbitrarily selected elements of that motion; but at the same time, a large proportion of human error comes from the arbitrary division of continuous motion into discontinuous elements."

Leo Tolstoy
War and Peace

Principles of How Organizations Work

Four basic principles explain how organizations work: (1) acceptance of people as the organization, (2) strategic alignment, (3) interdependency, and (4) congruency. Used together, they become powerful tools to predict and manage the change essential to building flexible organizations.

❑ People centeredness is understanding that organizations are the people that comprise them. They are groups of people organized to accomplish a specific purpose.

❑ Strategic alignment is the fit between an organization's purpose, strategy, and its market place. It is the organizational equivalent of building a sleek and fast racing boat to sail competitively versus building a comfortable and slow day sailer for touring.

   In flexible organizations, strategic alignment means that organizational purpose and strategy must change when the dynamics of the market change or customers' needs change.

❑ Interdependency describes the dependent, interconnected relationship between all the components of an organization. A change in one component changes all the others.

3

❏   Congruency is the fit between the internal components of an organization. The better the fit, the better the organization functions.

People Centeredness

A fundamental tenet of current management theory is that employees are the organization's "greatest assets."[1] This concept has developed
over the last twenty years to stress the important and critical role that
employees play in today's organizations. It is a major paradigm shift from
those that preceded it. During the Industrial Revolution people were
regarded as interchangeable, replaceable cogs in the organizational
machine. Companies required people to act as machines, supplying
mechanical labor. Workers were encouraged not to think, or make judgments about ways to make products. They were only to do. It was a belief
that fit its time and enabled the great industrialists to build the foundation
for today's economy. This mechanistic paradigm fit its time as the "people are assets" paradigm fits the post-industrial, post-World War II era.
But times keep changing.

All organizations revolve around what the people think and dream,
what they can do and what they cannot do, what their backgrounds are
and what their backgrounds are not. Apple emerged from Steve Job's
dreams, and his ability to tinker with electronics. Marketing-driven firms
require people who are experienced marketers, complemented by people
with other business skills. Organizations have all the potential and all the
limitations of the people in them. Equipment, systems, technologies,
products and services are all created by people and used by them to
accomplish specific tasks and purposes. People are the brain of the organization viewed as a living, dynamic organism.

The development of the personal computer ushered in the
Information Age, where data is no longer a limited commodity and information is available to everyone. The requirements of the Information Age,
and its successor, the Knowledge Age,[2] have outdated the people-are-
assets paradigm. The Information Age requires that companies populate

---

[1] See *Harvard Business Review,* "People: Managing Your Most Important Asset," 1988.

[2] Presented by Dr. Stanley M. Davis at the *Human Resource Planning Society's* 1993
Annual Conference. For further information see Dr. Stanley's *Twenty Twenty Vision,*
published by Simon and Schuster, 1992.

themselves with people who can interpret and analyze data, turn it into knowledge, and then use their judgment to act.

Consequently, companies that are competing in the Information Age require a new paradigm for the role of people in organizations. To be able to succeed in the increasingly competitive global market place, companies must encourage people to learn, to think, and to act independently of managers and supervisors whose role was to control them. They need a paradigm that enables executives to harness and orchestrate the ability, judgment, and experience of the employees of the organization.

In the Information Age, people are not assets. They cannot be depreciated on the books, nor can they be warehoused for later use. When not actively involved in the daily work of the company, they grow stale and rigid, unusable in flexible, fast-paced organizations. Conversely, organizations without people are not organizations. They are collections of equipment, bank accounts earning interest, buildings for lease, and stocks of products for sale. Organizations are the people who populate them. Individuals, dyads, triads, and teams are the driving force behind anything and everything that an organization has done, can do, or will do. In short, people are the center of the organization.

Impact of the People-Centered Organization®
Paradigm Shift: The Role Of Management

Viewing organizations as people-centered shifts the management paradigm from controlling people to developing and guiding within an organizational system, consistent with the needs of the Information and Knowledge Ages. The people-centered paradigm shifts the role of management from operating the organizational machine or protecting the company's assets. Rather it demands they lead and guide interconnected groups of adults, who have the inherent ability to think, analyze, and determine their own actions. Controlling fits the old paradigm of replaceable cogs and people as assets, stifling individual judgment and creativity. Leading and guiding emphasizes the unique contribution that everyone must make in today's organizations.

The People-Centered Organization® paradigm shift enables executives to focus on five key concepts central to building and managing flexible organizations:

1. Developing and using vision, mission, and values as organizational "glue" to build cohesiveness;
2. Leading, orchestrating, developing, and inspiring people as the new role of executives and managers;
3. Creating a learning organization;
4. Continually assessing organizational capabilities; and
5. Leading and managing continuous change.

These five concepts become the guidelines for managing, describing what management does, in People-Centered Organizations®. Individuals in Knowledge era companies need direction, leadership, information, challenges, and the freedom to continually adapt.[3] They do not need what traditional management typically has provided: strategic mystery, control, limited information, routine, and repetition.

Today's successful executives understand this seismic shift. While they focus on providing the five concepts to their companies, they have dropped authority and responsibility to the lowest possible levels and to those closest to the problem. They have recognized a fundamental truth about People-Centered Organizations®—get out of the way and let those who know the job best do it.

Vision, Mission, and Values as Organizational Glue

Individuals plan and control their own lives. They direct their actions based on their values and beliefs, taking action willfully and purposefully.[4] Individuals are continually seeking a balance between their own identity as an individual and their identity as a member of a group.[5] They seek to find a purpose as individuals and as members of a group. Because people are purpose-driven, People-Centered Organizations® are purpose-driven. Purpose, therefore, is an organizational glue that binds people together. They share a common purpose, with an ensuing set of objectives that provide a common base for understanding each other's actions.

---

[3] See Frederick Hertzberg, *Harvard Business Review*, "People: Managing Your Most Important Asset," 1988. "One More Time: How Do You Motivate Employees?", pp. 26-35, 1988.

[4] See Otto Rank, *The Trauma of Birth*, London: Paul, Trench, Truber & Co., and Harcourt and Brace, 1929.

[5] See Otto Rank, *Will Therapy and Truth and Reality*, translated by Jessie Taft. New York: Alfred Knopf, 1947.

People need to know and understand why they must perform certain tasks and what the consequences will be. Understanding is essential if they are to perform as adults, as capable, intelligent humans. Understanding purpose is one type of organizational "glue" that helps bind people together. The People-Centered Organization® paradigm enables executives to see more clearly that purpose is essential; without most employees understanding an organization's purpose and direction, there is no organizational purpose.

Shared values and beliefs[6] are a second type of organizational "glue," tying people together. High-performing work groups typically have a strongly held set of values that set performance and behavior expectations, reducing the need for traditional organizational control mechanisms.[7] When organizations are viewed as people-centered, then executives can more readily see the importance and role of values and beliefs.

Executives and managers who understand the importance of organizational glue spend most of their time focusing on the big picture issues of direction and values. They excel at communicating it throughout the company. Most importantly, they listen. They listen to the reaction of the staff and make modifications based on what they hear. They listen to the companies' customers and the market places sounds, shifting strategies and tactics to leverage unique opportunities.

Leading, Orchestrating, and Inspiring

People-Centered Organization® executives lead and orchestrate the natural flows within the company. They understand that they must rise above the daily detail, anticipate the business needs of the company, sense the emotional tenor of the staff, and stretch the capabilities of the organization. Like an outstanding orchestra conductor, they must understand the desires of the audience, demand superb performance from the musicians, and weave together the notes to create a new interpretation of success.

---

[6] See Stephen R. Covey, *The Seven Habits of Highly Effective People,* New York: Simon and Schuster, 1989.

[7] See Edward W. Lawler, *High Involvement Organizations,* San Francisco: Jossey-Bass Inc., 1986.

They also understand that simply creating an ethical, worthwhile purpose for a company is insufficient. Executives must lead and guide by living the articulated values and role modeling behavior consistent with the vision, mission and values. The company's purpose and values must be translated into behavioral action starting with them, then be spread throughout the organization.

Behavior, the most visible aspect of an individual's organizational life, is a much discussed key to leading today. Employees and managers are aware of executive behavior, continually observing and interpreting their leaders' actions. They are keenly aware of when an executive lives up to the standards in the company's philosophy statement. They are angry and disappointed when an executive fails to maintain the standards, or when an executive requires different behavior from some managers and not others.

Leading by example exerts moral force, and demonstrates that executives understand that organizational purpose is greater than any individual's purpose. It sets an expectation that people will all strive for the same goal within a defined set of values.

Creating Learning Organizations

Using the People-Centered Organization® paradigm enables management to more easily see the need for continual employee education and development. If organizations are to be continually changing, then the employees must be continually learning and growing. Individually, most people do not grow on a linear basis; they do not learn in a predetermined, syllabus sequence. Rather, they seek learning experiences as they need them, acquiring the knowledge and skill to solve a particular problem or understand an issue. Consequently, executives in flexible organizations have learned that employee development must be broad enough to allow individuals to explore and grow, while maintaining a focus on the organizational purpose. Motorola's University's employee development is built on this concept and has proven its success.

Assessing Organizational Capabilities

The People-Centered Organization® paradigm also enables executives to view organizational capabilities in a new light. When designing the organization of the future, the question to ask is not "**what** do we want to be," but rather "**who** do we want to be." "Who do we want to be" emphasizes the intellectual assets of a company and the institutional learning and experience that have become the key in competitive, volatile markets. "What we want to be" emphasizes the mechanistic model, the "we can assemble the parts approach." Viewing organizations as "who do we want to be" also reinforces that the organization is a whole that is greater then the sum of its parts. Everyone within the organization has a stake in how it runs and what it accomplishes. It validates and gives form to thinking of the various organizational constituents as stakeholders.

To cite an example, a major professional services firm revised its strategy from selling to all clients in its market to selling only to the top tier. The partners decided to reach this market by changing to "who they were" rather than "what they were." Consequently, they changed the firm's hiring patterns, shifting from hiring high performers in good schools to hiring outstanding performers from the five top graduate schools in the US. The partners were clear that who was employed defined what the firm was.

Leading and Managing Continuous Change

The People-Centered Organization® framework also reinforces the concept that organizations do not change, people do. Many company executives have been frustrated in attempts to change their organizations when they ran into "people" problems. They had crafted well-conceived strategies that were based on the assumption that as soon as the changes were announced, the employees would immediately shift to the new ways of working. They were surprised that employees resisted the change because they had failed to view the organization as people centered.

It is only when executives view the organization as the people in it, that they begin to understand that organizations change in exactly the same manner that people change. Organizations can change as quickly or as slowly as people perceive the need to change and have the ability to change. Controlling change in the people-centered organizational framework is an oxymoron. Control, adjust, tweak, force, or tinker are verbs that describe mechanistic approaches to change. Lead, guide, influence, persuade, or coach are verbs for people-centered organizations.

Executives lead organization change by defining the purpose of the organization, identifying the need to change, and enabling the employees to make the necessary changes to support the new organizational direction. They accomplish it by creating an organizational environment of continuous learning, in which thinking, using individual judgment, and taking action are the expected norms. They lead change by orchestrating and influencing those around them.

Strategic Alignment

Strategic alignment is the way in which organizations shape themselves to meet the needs of their markets and customers. For example, a defense contracting company's purpose is to provide the products and services that the military needs, at a profit to the company's shareholders. The executives, managers, and employees fulfill this purpose by identifying and understanding the needs of the military and developing business strategies to meet these requirements. The military's needs change as world politics shift and the company's executives anticipate this shift by preparing for growth during times of rearmament, and diversifying in times of retrenchment, that is, aligning themselves with the changing market.

Markets continually change and companies' strategies change with market shifts. Like dance partners, companies and markets have a reciprocal relationship. Either can lead or they can take turns leading, but they must be in step with each other. However, unlike dance partners, where both lose when one falls out of step with the other, the company loses and the market finds a new partner. If the company falls out of step, then it is penalized. When the company leads it must be aware of where the market is. It must not move two steps ahead or it will trip up its partner, losing its customers in the market by being too far ahead and being replaced by a company that more accurately anticipated the marketplace. When the market leads, the company must remain in step or at worst, a step behind. Dropping two steps behind again penalizes the company, as customers shift their purchases to other companies in step with the market.

The marketplace is comprised of many markets so that it can dance with many different companies at the same time. The many partners dance to different music, but each will dance within the parameters of leading or following. Some dance to jazz, some to the blues, and some to a fox-trot. Deliberately, each couple dances differently, following a conscious or unconscious strategy to win the contest that they all are entered in.

Dancing in the Marketplace

Two companies in the same market but in different niches in the toy retailing business provide clear and more detailed examples of this principle. FAO Schwartz occupies an upscale, exclusive market, catering to the wealthy. It's strategy is to maintain an extensive stock of exclusive toys, mix the stock liberally with popular toys, provide a high degree of service, and charge the highest possible prices. FAO Schwartz markets nationally and internationally and has created a brand name aura. In short, the strategy is high quality, high volume, high service, and high margins.

In Southern New Jersey, a discount toy store locally nicknamed "Dirty Harry's" (in reality named Discount Harry's) has developed the opposite strategy. "Dirty Harry's" offers a large stock of the most popular toys at the lowest possible prices with the least amount of service. The store is in two warehouse type buildings a few minutes drive outside Philadelphia. "Dirty Harry's" is virtually a drive-in retail store. No frills, no gimmicks, no eye catching displays, just rows and rows of toys that the customer can grab, pay for, and leave. The strategy is clearly high volume, low margins.

Each company is in strategic alignment with its market niche. Each has built a strategy that meets the demands of its market. FAO Schwartz overwhelms the customer with magnificent displays of thousand-dollar stuffed animals. "Dirty Harry's" underwhelms the customer with row after row of dull, steel shelves filled with deeply discounted games, dolls, and sporting equipment. FAO Schwartz's employees are impeccably dressed, unfailingly polite (by New York city standards), and provide toy expertise upon request. "Dirty Harry's" employees wear rumpled clothes, frequently do not respond when asked a question, and only provide information about items when pressed to respond.

Each of these retailers has built a powerful, profitable, and loyal customer base. Each has developed a retail strategy to meet the needs and expectations of their customers in their market niche. If their niche changes, then so must they. Conversely, if their niche does not change, neither can they. "Dirty Harry's" tried to make a shift to a more upscale market several years ago, seemingly an easy move to make. The employees swept and polished the floors, rearranged the shelves so that the toys were neatly stacked and organized, began to answer customer questions, and in general acted as if they worked at Toys "R" Us. The change so startled their customers that business quickly dropped off. No one could believe that the prices were no longer the lowest possible, for in the customer's mind, good service and cleanliness translated to higher prices.

Both these retailers demonstrate that executives must understand the dynamics of their market, determine their market niche, and develop a strategy to reach that niche. Executives need to identify the right strategy for their company at any given moment and be prepared to switch if and when the market dynamics change. They must learn to dance with the market.

How Marketplace Dancing has Changed

The link between market realities, organizational purpose, and strategy demands is the foundation of the art and science of designing and leading organizations. When market realities remain stable over a significant period of time, as they did for the automotive industry during the 1950 and 1960's, then the link between market and strategy remains stable and needs no change. However, in periods of shifting market realities and changing strategies, organizational purpose and strategy must be changed to meet the new market realities.

For most of the twentieth century, the primary goal of the successful corporation was to create stability, institutionalize routine, and manage procedures. Overlooked during this period of strategic stability, was the historical pattern of organizational form following function.[8] Business history is filled with success stories built around matching organizational form to function.

The well-established giants of the twentieth century were designed to maximize the advantage of pursuing this goal. Thomas Watson, Sr., built IBM to dominate the market by offering high-quality products with superior and informed service. He created a company culture that centered on being the largest and the best, and supported that by ensuring that IBM treated all its employees in the best manner possible, consistent with the times. In its prime, IBM was not monolithic and ponderous, but rather a growing corporation that used its size and strengths to execute a well-conceived strategy. IBM was not built for the ages, but rather for its particular market and times.

---

[8] See Tom Burns and G. M. Stalker, *The Management of Change,* Chicago: Quadrangle Books, 1962. Also see Jane Woodward, *Industrial Organization: Theory and Practice,* London: Oxford Press, 1965.

Conventional wisdom from the 1930's to the early 1980's was that the large manufacturing organization was right for its time. But it was not right for all times. Organizations must shift with the market place, anticipating and meeting market needs and demands in the most efficient and effective manner possible. For almost half a century the traditional organization was highly successful, but the late 1980's and early 1990's have proven that times have changed. Executives no longer have the luxury of building stable, unchanging organizations in which everyone has time to understand, learn, and improve their performance. The markets are so volatile that organizations must continually flex to meet new needs, match new competition, and create new products and services.

Interdependency

Most executives and managers intuitively understand that all aspects of the organization are interrelated and that a change in one creates a change in all the others. This principle is a basic tenet of systems theory, originally developed to explain interrelatedness in biological systems.[9] Organizations, as living systems, respond to change throughout.

A key characteristic of any living system is its ability to adapt, to respond to a change in the environment by changing itself to match the environment. The process of adaptation usually requires that the organism make multiple changes to the environmental stimulus. The changes are interconnected and can be easily viewed as tradeoffs. Life cycle changes in a family readily illustrate this principle. Parents often cherish the responsibility and gratification of caring for a baby. The baby is responsive, warm, loving, and usually appreciative of any and all attention and care she receives. The parents enjoy the immediate gratification of taking care of a baby's needs, however, the tradeoff for the parents is significant. They have less time for themselves, are on call twenty-four hours a day, and have no choice but to respond to the baby's cry.

The tradeoff principle holds true no matter what life cycle stage the family is in. When the baby grows into a teenager, she can do a lot more to meet her own needs and is less dependent on her parents. In fact, she can take responsibility for activities that her parents used to do, setting the

---

[9] See James G. Miller, "Living Systems: The Organization." *Behavioral Science* 17 (1) (January 1972) for a comprehensive discussion.

table, cooking some of the meals, mowing the lawn, and washing the car. The tradeoff remains in affect. Parents worry about having less control than they had previously, wondering if she is safe at the dance, or on the canoe trip. They have to learn how to deal with challenges to their authority and decide how much independence their child should have. They have gained relief from some of the carekeeping but lost much of the gratification of caring for a baby.

The interdependency principle holds true for all aspects of organizational life. For example, on a strategic level, the executive team of a small manufacturer of specialty coatings for the pharmaceutical industry decided that the company needed to develop new products to offset a potential decline in current products. They decided to bring to the market a new process that they had some success in experimenting with on several previous jobs. They shifted the time allocation of the R&D engineer and her staff from improving quality on current products to developing the new product.

The R&D staff had more difficulty in developing the product than anticipated, and while their time was spent in developing the new product, the quality of the current products slipped. Sales dropped and the executive team had to cut personnel to make the budget balance. The executives laid off an R&D staff member and the new product development process slowed down even more. Finally, the executives re-allocated the R&D engineer's time back to quality improvement to maintain current sales. The executive team had failed to see the tradeoff that they were making when they decided to make the original change.

The tradeoff, unintentionally made, was to sacrifice current product quality for the more rapid introduction of a new process. If the executive team had been aware that they were making a tradeoff, they could have anticipated the consequences and managed them. Organizational life, like family life, is a set of tradeoffs that needs to be accepted as reality and managed.

Conversely, the executive team of the corporate service department of a Fortune 50 company anticipated a shift in the department's role as the company adjusted to massive changes in the market place. The executives decided to shift the department's role from monitoring and policing divisional activities to providing expertise to the divisions. The executives understood that making this type of change would alter every aspect of the department. Consequently, as they shifted the role of the department, they created task forces to revise job descriptions, evaluation processes, hiring and firing policies, and supervisory roles. They coordinated the work of the task forces so that changes recommended by one task force were reviewed by all the others and after negotiation between the task forces, each incorporated all the changes into their work. The executives understood the interplay between all aspects of the department and created a process that managed the tradeoffs.

Understanding interrelatedness is a key to building flexible organizations. Executives cannot build flexible organizations unless they develop processes and systems that manage, monitor, and realign the tradeoffs made as one area of an organization shifts and impacts on another.

Congruency

Congruency occurs when organizations have all their components aligned with each other. The components fit together, reinforcing and supporting each other. Congruency is a dynamic process, a shifting interchange among organizational components as each responds to changes in the whole and to changes within itself.

The interplay in the tidal marsh is a good example of this shifting and interchange inherent in organizational congruency. When the tide is in, the mussels and shells that live on the edge of the water are able to feed on the nutrients in the water. They open their shells to allow the water to run through them so they can strain the nutrients from the water. When the tide is out, the mussels and shells become food for the birds and mammals that live in the tidal marsh. They respond to the environmental danger by closing their shells, burying in the tidal mud, and hiding from their predators. The various organisms that live in the marshes are aligned to the tidal rhythms, synchronized with the ebb and flow of life. They shift their activities to match that of their environment. The very long-lived organisms are also able to adapt to major disturbances in their environment. Each has a well developed strategy to survive in its environment and realigns itself to the changes or disturbances in its environment in order to thrive.

Ideally, organizations act in the same way. They have a marketplace strategy that allows them to thrive and they align their components to enable them to implement their strategy. Their components are in a dynamic state of congruency, shifting to meet the normal shifts in the market. They must be able to support the strategy to thrive in their niche and they must have a well-developed, successful strategy.

Like their counterparts on the tidal marshes, they risk extinction when they do not adapt to the environment. Two major maladaptions can occur. First, executives may choose the wrong strategy or set of strategies, a failure of alignment. Second, executives may fail to create and maintain internal consistency, a failure of congruence.

When organizations are unaligned their organizational structures and processes may be internally consistent, but their strategy is not aligned to market realities. When "Dirty Harry's" realigned its internal form to provide cleaner, better service, it may have been organizationally congruent but its strategy of attracting upscale customers was not aligned with its market realities. No matter how congruent the organization may have been, it could not overcome failing to meet its customers' expectations. Organizational congruency is essential to flexible organizations, but will not alone produce high functioning. Organizations must be both strategically aligned and congruent.

When organizations are aligned but not performing well, they are most often incongruent. The specialty coatings manufacturer, discussed earlier, developed a good strategy. It was correct in anticipating the market. It understood what it could do to meet the shift in the market, and it developed a plan to implement its strategy. Unfortunately, it was incongruent.

If viewed as a snapshot in time, most companies are partially out of alignment and partially incongruent. They are frozen in transition at a single point of time. The snapshot catches them attempting to respond to changes in the environment. The danger lies not in being unaligned or incongruent, but in staying that way, in being trapped partially in alignment and congruency and partially out.

For example, a snack food manufacturer had established itself as a regional presence in its market. The company's strategy had been to produce high quality, moderately priced snacks for Mom and Pop stores throughout the region. Company drivers/salespeople distributed the products, developing long term relationships with their customers, understanding each customer's market. As intended, they became an integral part of their customer's operation. The drivers/salespersons were surrounded by a congruent organization that matched the intimate feel of their customer relationships, providing individualized billing, custom orders, and special delivery when needed. The company treated the drivers/salespersons as they treated their customers, anticipating their needs and finding ways to make them more successful. Company management emphasized that the drivers/salespeople had to make a profit and receive the appropriate services from the company so that everyone could be successful.

The company became very successful and profitable. Then, the snack food market shifted as strong regional competitors grew big enough to market nationally and began to force the regional companies to compete on price. Frito-Lay and Eagle Brand snack foods began to compete in all the regional markets and forced the company's executive team to shift its strategy. It decided to try to grow large enough to compete nationally. They developed a two-step strategy, expanding to supermarkets in the region, then building regional presence in areas where Frito Lay and Eagle were the weakest. They expanded the production facility, hired marketing and distribution executives, and began to successfully penetrate the supermarkets.

Unfortunately, the company's organizational congruency supported the Mom and Pop market, not the regional supermarket or national markets. The executive team did not realize this at first. The company could and did stretch to service the regional supermarkets. The stretch was uncomfortable and shaky. While service and relationships were the competitive advantage in the Mom and Pop market, they were not in the regional market. At this point in the market, price was the dominant competitive advantage. The company began to lose market share in its core Mom and Pop business, but did not change internally to support the new regional supermarket business. The attempt at regionalization and nationalization failed because the congruency did not match the new strategy. Within eighteen months, the company was on the verge of bankruptcy.

Compensating For The Lack Of Strategic Alignment

When organizations have unclear or ill-defined strategies, the organization will frequently become congruent around some other defining characteristic. The characteristics vary depending on how long there has been a lack of a clarified strategy, the previous strategy, and the market dynamics. Organizations without direction create their own direction, then shift congruency to support the new direction. The railroad industry illustrates this well. When the interstate highway system and the national airlines matured enough to drain traffic and shipping from the railroads, most of the big railroad companies lost their strategic direction. The railroads had excelled at growing and building, at becoming bigger and better to serve an increasing volume of traffic. Executive teams were unclear about a strategy to survive and tried to operate in the old mode, however, without a clear direction, survival became the predominant strategy. The federal government increased its regulation to try to keep the railroads alive and the unions featherbedded in an attempt to protect their members' jobs. The railroad companies quickly became large bureaucracies whose major purpose was to exist. And, not surprisingly, all the components of the organization shifted to a new bureaucratic congruency.

Chapter Two
People-Centered Organizations

> "This book is about the organization man . . . it is they (sic) who are the mind and soul of our great self-perpetuating institutions."
>
> William Hollingsworth White
> *The Organization Man*

Flexible organizations are organizations that continuously change to meet new or different market and customer needs. Consequently, building and managing flexible organizations requires that executives learn how to manage continuous change. Learning how to build and manage flexible organizations requires that executives know:

❏ How organizations will respond internally to new strategies,

❏ How to manage the predicted and unpredicted internal responses to the strategic change, and

❏ How to maintain congruency and rebalance the organization components as they continually adjust and shift. Maintaining congruency is essential if an organization is to be able to respond rapidly to marketplace shifts.

To be able to build flexible organizations, executives need a practical framework that enables them to easily understand and apply the fundamental concepts discussed in Chapter 1. Executives need to be able to apply people-centeredness, strategic alignment, interdependency, and congruency to the specifics of their companies. The People-Centered Organizations® framework meets this need.

The People-Centered Organization® framework has seven interactive components: genetic core; philosophy; formal organization; information, technology, and work processes; behavior; informal organization; and culture. Each of the components is an organizational sub-system that is interdependent and interactive with the other six components. Each component needs to be congruent with the others and, together, all seven need to be congruent with the organization's strategy.

People-Centered Organization®

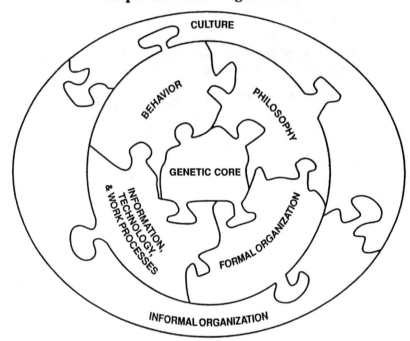

Drawing #1

1. The **genetic core** is the individual or the group of people who are the locus of power, the decision makers.
2. The **philosophy** is the publicly stated and articulated values and beliefs of the organization that emanate from the genetic core.
3. The **formal organization** is the set of hierarchical structures, reporting relationships, reward systems, and the control systems.
4. The **information, technology, and work processes** component is the set of constraints and demands of the technologies and processes, and the work steps, that determine daily operations and the links that provide the information for decision making.
5. The **behavior** component is the set of interactions between individuals and groups within the organization.
6. The **informal organization** is the network of friendships, acquaintances, similar backgrounds and alliances that link people together.
7. The **culture** is the normative set of beliefs of how the organization operates.

    The first five are the inner components that can be directly influenced and altered. The last two, the informal organization and culture, reflect the interplay and congruency between the inner five. See Drawing #1.

The Genetic Core

Cuius regio eius religio
(He who controls the area controls the religion)

Proverb

The genetic core is at the center of the People-Centered Organization® framework. As the name implies, the genetic core is analogous to an individual's genetic double-helix. In an individual, the DNA double-helix carries the genes that create the person. The genes determine an individual's gender, personality, talents, appearances, and preferences. These genetic predispositions are enhanced or diminished by the individual's life experiences and environment, but they provide the basic working tools for all individuals.

In an organization, the genetic core imprints its biases, beliefs, perceptions, and background on the entire organization. These predispositions unfold over time, triggered by internal and external events, influencing everyone in the organization. Sometimes the genius of the genetic core starts the whole organization, and at other times it revives a dying company. Sometimes the predispositions of men and women in the genetic core inspire and raise the performance of the employees. At other times, the predispositions create dysfunction and chaos, contributing to the demise of a company.

Examples of this abound. Steven Jobs at Apple was a brilliant entrepreneur and innovator. He used his technical genius to create the personal computer, then used his entrepreneurial abilities to found and build Apple. His abilities allowed him to create a company, but not to manage a corporation. Because he was not a manager, he had to step aside to allow a more experienced and capable manager, John Scully, to run the bigger company.

Thomas Watson, Sr., was a good salesman prior to joining IBM, but he was not an entrepreneur or an inventor. He was, however, a brilliant executive and manager whose true ability blossomed when he joined and managed IBM. He had a genius for organization and culture building that he embedded in the company and its employees.

Like individuals, organizations are born with inherent strengths and weaknesses. Initially, these predispositions are extensions of the founder's personal philosophy, behavior, beliefs, values, background, and abilities. These predispositions become the genes of the organization, embedded in the organizational processes and daily operations. The predispositions of the founders—the genes of the genetic core—determine the organization's initial capabilities, its focus, its character.

The external forces that existed at the organization's founding also become embedded in the organization's genes. Market dynamics, the prevailing cultural beliefs, the economy, and the technological capabilities of the times, as seen through the eyes of those in the genetic core, become embedded in the organization. IBM, again, is a good example of this principle. Thomas Watson, Sr., and Thomas Watson, Jr., were so skillful at creating and building a powerful organizational culture that when IBM needed to shift away from its genetic legacy, it could not make the shift without major upheaval.

The genetic core creates a genetic code that becomes the most significant force within the organization. The genetic code shapes the philosophy, the reporting relationships, the nature of the communication, and the behavior of the employees. It is a major factor in creating the organizational culture and even influences how the employees relate to each other. In the People-Centered Organizational framework, the genetic core directly influences the philosophy, the formal organization, the information, technology and work processes, and the behavior components. It also influences, to a lesser extent, the informal organization and the culture.

Ultimately, this genetic code influences how employees feel about the company and impacts upon their self-image. Immersed in the day to day life of the organization, employees learn how the organization "thinks and feels" about pertinent business issues. Like people living in a foreign country and culture, they begin to understand and appreciate the logic and perspective of the culture they are living in. If they stay in the country long enough, they slowly adopt some of the cultural attitudes as their own.

Most employees adopt some of the beliefs and attitudes of the organization they work in. Because much of the organizational attitude flows from the genetic core, employees are soon imprinted by the genetic code. Consequently, the genetic core has the power to profoundly influence how employees do their work, how they feel about their work, and how they feel about themselves. The organization centers on the genetic core.

How the Genetic Core Changes

The genetic core changes in three ways by: (1) the unfolding of the current occupants predispositions over time, (2) the infusion of new genetic core members, and (3) a significant change in the perceptions, beliefs, or attitudes of the genetic core members. Like an individual, the organization too is significantly altered by each of these changes, while retaining its basic character.

Turner Broadcasting System (TBS) changes in the last ten years illustrate how an owner's predispositions unfold over time and change the corporation. As Ted Turner grew in wealth and power, and as he matured, his predisposition for power grew from playing on an international scale to influencing international politics. Turner grew from sailing and winning the America's cup to building relations with Soviet Russia. In the mid-eighties, he began to take advantage, along with a few others, of the change in US-USSR relations. Capitalizing on a slight thaw in US-USSR relations, he created the Goodwill games as a non-Olympic year world sporting event. By creating a new world spectacle, he was able to position TBS as a global company, upstage his competitors, and positively influence the US-USSR relationship. He was able to combine his emerging need to be a global figure with his business acumen to position his company to become a global leader.

Infusing new genetic core members into the organization may be the most prevalent way organizations change. Any change in the genetic core is a significant indication that a major change is happening. Boards of Directors often replace CEOs and executives as a clear message that they expect significant change in the organization and its performance. CEOs frequently replace executive team members as an indication that the organization must change its strategy or improve in a key area. Companies add new genetic core members to prepare or manage new enterprises, new directions, or new opportunities. Regardless of the reason Boards or CEOs make the change, altering the genetic core creates a fundamental change in the organization.

IBM fired William Akers, bringing in Lou Gerstner to manage the massive changes that needed to be made if it was to survive. The IBM

Board did not believe that an insider would be able to drastically down-size the work force, replace competent but culturally blind executives, and change IBM's image in the marketplace. Changing CEOs, altering the genetic core, signaled the Board's willingness to make major changes to all IBM's major stakeholders—the stockholders, customers, and employees, as well as Wall Street.

Dun and Bradstreet adds genetic core talent before acquiring or moving to a new market as a regular management methodology. Once the executive team decides to enter a new market, they search for an executive who has experience in the market or industry to lead the effort to enter the market or acquire a new company. His or her job is twofold; bringing industry or market expertise to the existing genetic core, and using the wisdom and experience of the genetic core to assist in acquiring and integrating the new opportunity.

Bill Gates of Microsoft understood the need to add to the genetic core to manage new opportunities. As Microsoft grew beyond being a successful entrepreneurial company to become a late twentieth-century giant, Gates hired financial and managerial talent to add skills that he did not have. He understood that the organization needed more than he was capable of and so added the missing knowledge bases, skills, and perceptions by hiring competent, respected executives to manage key functions in the company. Consequently, Microsoft continues to thrive, still dependent on his visions of the world, but independent of his managerial skills.

Genetic core attitudinal changes are frequently less visible than other types of genetic core changes. Executives and Board members, like other individuals, grow and change with the times, and their growth can often be seen indirectly. When the General Electric Board settled on Jack Welch as Chairman, they were clear that GE had to shed its bureaucracy and become more responsive to the marketplace. They realized that GE needed to commit to long-term change. Consequently, they chose a young man, Jack Welch, who was an insider and who understood and valued many of the strengths of GE, to lead the change. He would be in the chairman's chair for a long time and would be able to drive the change without fear of being replaced. His hiring symbolized a change in attitude of the genetic core, the Board. Regardless of how or why a change is made to the genetic core, the current members must understand that they inherit the legacy of their predecessors. They can choose to build on the legacy, alter it, remove it, or deny it. Regardless of their choice, they blend their views, backgrounds, and capabilities with the legacy, in order to direct the organization.

Philosophy

"O philosophy, you leader of life."

Marcus Tullius Cicero
Tusculanae Disputationes

"By moral influence I mean that which causes the people to be in harmony with their leaders, so that they will accompany them in life and unto death without fear of moral peril."

Sun Tzu
The Art of War

Organizational philosophies, whether publicly stated or not, have always existed. Most often, they are the business beliefs and values of the genetic core. Employees have always known that what the CEO believes in is what the organization believes in and what they will be asked to believe in. Every time a new CEO is hired, the employees begin to discuss what she believes in, who she favors, what she thinks makes a successful organization, what she believes her role is, and of course, what will she think of them.

Prior to the mid-1980's, philosophies were generally unwritten. A few companies had publicly-stated mission statements and a brief statement of what the company stood for. But most companies simply had strategies that specified the markets they were in, the markets they wanted to be in, and how they planned to enter and succeeded in these markets. Executives communicated the strategies to the managers and employees, sharing the goals and objectives of the company with them. The shared strategies were assumed to be sufficient to motivate employees.

However, as markets became more global, more competitive, companies changed their basic approach to employment. Executives found that they needed less employees to do the basic tasks. They found that they needed more responsible employees who were willing to make decisions, use their judgment, and apply their business experience to complicated and crucial issues. Consequently, they delegated authority and responsibility to lower levels in the organization. They quickly discovered that managers and employees needed to know how and when to use newly delegated authority and responsibility. They needed to know what were the philosophical guidelines, what were the values that proscribed the expected behavior in the company.

Executives learned that one of the tradeoffs for asking more of managers and employees was that they would have to articulate a set of values that guided decision making. Additionally, they would have to role model the values to demonstrate that they believed in them and they expected everyone to live by them. And if they delegated the authority and responsibility, they could no longer control managers and employees by explicit, clearly stated goals. Therefore, they replaced the traditional methods of control with the more intangible and hopefully more powerful way of commonly held values.

Consequently, executive teams across the US and the world began to develop company vision, mission, and philosophy statements. These statements identified what the company hoped to be in the future, what its purpose was, and what the genetic core thought it should believe in to be successful. Most importantly, the philosophies identified a set of behavioral values, "shoulds" that identified ways that managers and employees should treat each other, customers, and other stakeholders.

A company's philosophy became an organizational glue that binds people together. The genetic core and all stakeholders of the organization measure the appropriateness of behavior, decisions, strategies, and actions by comparing them to the philosophy's "shoulds." As the power and influence of the traditional organization declines, the influence of the commonly held beliefs increases. Managers and employees looking for a job in today's market frequently search for a company that has values compatible with their own, looking to belong to an organization that shares similar beliefs.

Johnson & Johnson is an excellent example of a corporation with a clear and very strong statement of values that bind employees together. The

Johnson & Johnson Credo, created by the Johnson brothers over one hundred years ago, is consistently used as a key element in most decisions. It provides a unifying theme for the decentralized companies, enabling their executives to flex to local market dynamics without continually attempting to interpret what corporate headquarters would like them to do. No matter the industry, the global location, or the product, the Johnson & Johnson companies all are challenged to meet the standards of the credo.

Philosophies can also be a negative influence on an organization. If the genetic core articulates a philosophy and does not live up to its own standards, managers and employees quickly become cynical and disgruntled. A company's philosophy sets a standard that everyone affiliated with the organization must follow. If executives, managers, or employees are allowed to work outside the values, then the organizational glue begins to dry and flake, failing to bind people together.

For example, executives of a manufacturing company sought to implement new ways of working that required employees to assume more responsibility without an increase in salary. The CEO gave an impassioned speech to the twelve hundred employees asking them to make this sacrifice for the company so that it could survive in a more competitive marketplace. The CEO announced that the company was changing, becoming an enlightened, progressive employer, ready to challenge the future. The employees, though skeptical, responded to the challenge and using the new work processes, vastly improved productivity. Later, however, the employees felt betrayed when the CEO announced that he was giving only the executives extraordinary bonus because they alone knew how to think. Shortly after his comments and the bonuses became common knowledge, several fires broke out in the main manufacturing facility.

The Formal Organization

"Sometimes it is said that man cannot be trusted with government of himself. Can he, then, be trusted with the government of others?"

Thomas Jefferson
First Inaugural Address, March 4, 1801

The formal organization is the set of hierarchical structures, reporting relationships, reward systems, and control systems that organize and structure the organization. The formal organization's purpose is to identify:

- ❏ groups and individuals that perform specific roles;
- ❏ accountabilities and responsibilities;
- ❏ rewards and punishments;
- ❏ boundaries and limits;
- ❏ group and individual performance;
- ❏ the systems that monitor and control them.

For many, the formal organization is the road map that guides them through the organizational maze. It acts as the program for a baseball game, identifying who is who, and who plays where. It's key sub-components reveal further information about the player and the club, sharing current and past performance, future capabilities, individual and organizational aspirations. The organizational hierarchy indicates the formal decision makers, relative power among executives and managers, and each employee's status. The accounting system monitors and controls the money (and, therefore power) and indicates the relative importance of various projects and initiatives. Policy and procedures sets the behavioral standards and the use of the discipline system demonstrates what is tolerated and what is not tolerated.

The formal organization is also a highly visible symbol of management's intentions. It is a symbol of how things really are. No matter what management says about sharing responsibility and authority, until the organizational chart is drawn to reflect a sharing of power, few believe what management has promised. Employees skeptically listen to executive plans to empower lower levels of the organization, to institute cross-functional teams, and to increase employee participation in decision making. They seldom believe management's intention until they see visible, significant changes in the formal organization.

For example, a corporate services department in a Fortune 50 company had spent three years revamping the way it worked. The department shifted from strong hierarchical control to flattened, highly participative employee-management teams. Everyone in the department was involved in the change process, providing input into the department's vision, mission, and philosophy. Staff members were highly involved in task forces that redesigned all aspects of the department. Yet in a survey, the employees expressed a high degree of skepticism about management's intent to continue on the new course because the formal organizational chart still reflected the old, hierarchical organization.

The formal organization is the component that most employees, managers, and executives are comfortable with. It is the organizational component that is visible and tangible, and the easiest to change. It is the most comfortable to change because executives and managers are familiar with rearranging reporting relationships, changing policy and procedures, and revising budgets and plans. Making these changes may be complex, time demanding, and tiresome, but the methodology is familiar and known.

Unfortunately, executives frequently forget that any change in the formal organization triggers changes in the other components. A change in the pay systems will alter the organizational philosophy, strengthening the philosophy if it is consistent with it, and weakening it if it is inconsistent. The pay system changes will influence behavior, altering employees attitudes toward performing. Employees may have to change particular work processes to comply to the pay system changes and require additional information to perform the changed work processes. The change in the pay system ripples through the entire organization, creating unintended imbalances that reduce the intended impact.

Information, Technology, and Work Processes

"With his sixty years' experience he knew what value to attach to rumors, knew how apt people who desire anything are to group all news so that it appears to confirm what they desire, and he knew how readily in such cases they omit all that makes for the contrary."

Leo Tolstoy
War and Peace

"Since human social intelligence, tool use, and language all depend on quantitative increases in brain size and in it's associated information processing capacities, none could have suddenly emerged full-blown . . . These capacities are interdependent, none could have reached it's modern level of complexity in isolation."

Kathleen Gibson
Presentation to the Wenner-Gren Foundation for Anthropological Research March 1990

"A Journey of a thousand miles must begin with a single step."

Lao-tzu
The Way of Lau-tzu

The information, technology, and work processes component is the set of constraints and demands of the technologies and processes, and the work steps, that determine daily operations and the linkages that provide the information for decision making. Each aspect of this component either carries information or pushes forward the work that connects employees and produces goods and services. The purpose of the information, technology, and work processes component is to share, arrange, and shape information, products, and services.

It has three sub-components:

1. Formal communication channels that link people by conveying words, numbers, or other symbols;
2. Technologies that provide tools to enable people to perform tasks;
3. Work processes that are sets of tasks to complete a service or make a product.

The formal information channels criss-cross the organization, connecting employees through ideas, concepts, instructions, decisions, and desires. Most communication channels are either well established and routine—monthly departmental meetings—or flexible and based on need—one-on-one meetings on a particular topic. The channels run vertically, horizontally, and diagonally across the organization. The channels have many forms: memorandums, meetings, manuals, bulletin boards, E-mails, voice mails, newsletters, plans, white papers, and proposals.

In designing a flexible organization, the key issues in this sub-component are what information to share, how much information to share, who has access and which channel to use. Executives need to share as much information as is consistent with the strategic need and the philosophy. If the company desperately needs new products, then executives need to create access to the information that employees need to innovate. If a pipe manufacturer wants to encourage innovation at the machine operator level, then the operator needs access to information about the material composition and prices, customer need and specifications, and past product history.

An organization's technology is the set of tools used to accomplish specific tasks. Every organization is full of tools—computers, spray painters, drill presses, fork lifts, conveyor belts—and the employees are continually modifying and improving them. As with any tool, the technology enables employees to perform tasks in an efficient way, but also limits them at the same time. The word processing programs of the personal computer greatly enhance what a typist can do, but also limits him to seeing a partial page on the monitor screen. Pliers allow an employee to gain a greater grip on a pipe fitting, but limit her to the size of the pipe she can grab.

Technological characteristics influence all components of the organization. How fast the paint ovens can bake a finish determines how many car panels can be produced. How hot the oven is determines how warm the production area will be. How warm the production room is determines how comfortable workers will be. And the greater the discomfort of the employees, the higher the wages must be to attract workers.

The work processes, the set of steps required to accomplish a task, integrate the information required to do the task with the technology available to perform the task. Typically, the more information required, and the less sophisticated the technology, the greater the elapsed time required to complete a work process set. Work processes are frequently undocumented, particularly in the service industries, (hence the current popularity of re-engineering, the documenting and streamlining of the steps in a work process) and in many organizations, are considered to be sacred and only to be changed with great forethought and executive approval.

Changing work processes creates major changes in the organization. If management changes the work processes, then the corresponding technologies, information sharing, worker skills, and time constraints must change. Additionally, management should expect significant behavior changes in affected employees which must be anticipated and managed.

This type of change is a common one in today's organizations. When professionals first began to use personal and laptop computers to create documents, they complained about having to learn to type, of doing work that was beneath their status, and wasting their time. As they became proficient in word processing, they preferred creating their own documents because it removed time and communication constraints. After they became proficient, they began experimenting and competing with each other to find the best way to word process. The behavior change was immense, the impact on the organization great, and the work process changes were minor.

Behavior

"As with any ecosystem, the inhabitants whose behaviors and experiences are best suited to or fit the demands will be able to thrive; the inhabitants whose experience and behavior mismatch the ecosystem's demands will experience stress."

Carol H. And Stephen R. Lankton
Tales of Enchantment

Behaviors are the set of interactions between individuals and groups within the organization. The purpose of this component is to shape employee behavior to efficiently and effectively perform the work of the organization. Behavior is the most visible and most personal component of an organization, and frequently the component least managed. Behavior is the most personal component because it is the one we experience. We see it , we feel it, and we do it. It is the essence of every one-on-one and group interaction.

Because it is what we see, behavior is the indicator of what we believe people to be. Customers judge the nature and the quality of the employees' organization by their behavior. Customers make judgments about the organization's purpose and philosophy by the employees' behavior. Consequently, behavior must be consistent with the rest of the organization for customers to understand the organization's identity and purpose.

Behavior encompasses a multitude of interpersonal and group interactions such as: when people arrive to a meeting, how they behave at the meeting, how promptly they do assignments, how thoroughly they perform their tasks, and how well they treat each other. Behavior includes the way managers work with employees, with each other, and how employees treat managers. Diversity issues are partially included in this component, because the real issue in managing diversity is treating everyone fairly and equally, that is, managing behaviors.

Behavior is messy. Individuals perceive behavior differently. Behavior that is polite and acceptable in one culture may be thoroughly unacceptable and rude in another. Expressing strong feelings about an idea may be perfectly acceptable in an advertising agency but unacceptable in a pharmaceutical company. Individual behavior is frequently viewed differently by individuals of the same background and experiences. Behavior that is acceptable for one person, is not for another. Behavior always has gray areas that make some comfortable and others uncomfortable.

For example, a manager who storms out of a meeting may be viewed by her peers as determined and principled, domineering and spoiled, or just having a bad day. The interpretation is in the eye of the beholder. Because of its complexity, its intangibleness, and its messiness, it is the component that most managers ignore or avoid.

Organizational behavior is a paradox. Organizations are judged on their employees' behavior, but executives and managers are reluctant to deal directly with behavior. Instead, they attempt to change it indirectly by skill training, policy and procedures, and evaluation. The United States' labor laws also make direct intervention in behavior difficult, prescribing management behavior in hiring, firing, and evaluating. These legal limitations and constraints reinforce managers and executives' indirect efforts to change behavior.

Behavior is purposeful. Individuals choose to behave one way because they view it as a logical choice based on the information on hand. Most of the time behavior is rational, a deliberate choice of actions in response to their environment. If company policy requires employees to fill out time and expense reports promptly after company mandated travel, and the company reimburses the employees tardily, some staff will begin to mimic the tardiness of the organization by failing to file their reports promptly. In their eyes, they are simply responding to environmental cues that sanction lateness.

Consequently, executives and managers can use behavior as information that when pieced together reveals an organizational incongruity. If there is no incongruity, then they must begin to examine other factors that might cause the individual to behave in a manner seemingly inconsistent with organizational purpose and goals. In other words, when employees are not behaving in the expected fashion, first examine what the organization is doing to create the employee behavioral response. If organizational incongruities are not causing the response, then look for other reasons like team interaction or personal development issues.

Informal Organization

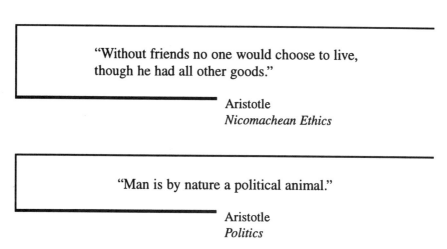

"Without friends no one would choose to live, though he had all other goods."

Aristotle
Nicomachean Ethics

"Man is by nature a political animal."

Aristotle
Politics

The informal organization is the network of friendships and acquaintances that link people together across departmental boundaries and through hierarchical levels. The informal organization is composed of loose alliances based on mutual self-interest, and joint membership in multiple groups. The purpose of the informal organization is twofold; (1) to provide a social network for employees, and (2) to act in the best interest of the employees.

In all organizations the informal organization component serves as a social network, providing a personal network as in any other community. The informal organization network allows people of like interests to share common social interaction within the organization. As a social network, it counterbalances the intensity and focus of working, allowing people to obtain a break from the daily pressures of the business.

Often, however, the informal organization fulfills a second purpose within organizations, counterbalancing dysfunction within or among the inner five components (genetic core, philosophy, formal organization, information, technology, and work processes, and behavior). In these situations, the informal organization mirrors the health of the organization. The healthier the organization, the more the informal organization acts a social network and less as a counterbalance. It supports and compliments the purpose of the organization. The less healthy the organization, the more the informal organization shifts to serving the interests of the individuals in the organization. In an unhealthy organization, the informal organization counterbalances the dysfunction of the rest of the organization in many ways. For example, by sharing information that informs the employees of critical information that they do not receive through formal channels, or by creating informal work processes to complete tasks.

If the organization has no strategic direction, then the informal organization replaces the lack of direction with an emphasis on maintaining job security. If the organization is too controlling and too stifling, the informal organization counterbalances by protecting the freedom of the individual. If the organization is too bureaucratic, the informal organization finds ways to circumvent the bureaucracy, ensuring that key tasks be completed quickly.

If the company is relatively functional and healthy, then the common purpose of the informal organization is communal, to be good and helpful neighbors. If the organization is dysfunctional and unhealthy, then the purpose of the informal organization shifts to meeting the needs of sub-group members. In heavily bureaucratic organizations, the informal organization often assists employees to find ways around the red tape to complete their assigned tasks. In highly dysfunctional organizations, employees use the informal organization to warn each other about impending negative events and to protect themselves from arbitrary negative behavior by management. In this type of organization, employees are not concerned with getting the job done, but simply protecting their jobs and avoiding the chaos of a mismanaged organization. In highly-compartmentalized organizations, the informal organization becomes the network to accomplish cross-departmental tasks.

The grapevine, the informal communication channels that connect individuals, is the communication process for the informal organization. It is the fastest and most far-reaching communication channel. News travels faster through the grapevine than any other channel in the organization. Information on the grapevine is quickly accepted as fact in most organizations, and indeed, is very accurate in most organizations. Employees tend to believe the information carried on the grapevine because it is not filtered by management, and because it is communicated by someone they know, a peer or a colleague. It is more personal, and therefore more believable. The most likely to be believed and the most vulnerable to distortion, even though it is often based on the truth.

Like the rest of the informal organization, the grapevine acts as a counterbalance to the formal communication channels. The counterbalancing rules are:

❑   the less information passed through formal communication channels, the more communication passes in the grapevine,

❑   the greater the uncertainty in the organization, the greater the volume in the grapevine;

❑   the more vague the formal organization channels, the more specific the grapevine; and

❑   the less personal the formal organization channels, the more personal the grapevine.

Culture

"It's not just what we inherit from our mothers and fathers that haunts us. It's all kinds of old defunct theories, all sorts of old, defunct beliefs, and things like that. It's not that they actually live on in us; they are simply lodged there, and we cannot get rid of them.

Henrik Ibsen,
Ghosts

The culture is the normative set of beliefs of how the organization operates. The culture is best described "as the way we really do things here." It is a combination of the way the organization strives to operate (philosophy), the way the organization has operated in the past (its legacy), and the way the organization operates at the moment. This blend of past, present and future creates the present culture.

Culture is highly intangible and like behavior, perceived differently by different viewers. A long-term employee, one who has worked in the company for over thirty years, will perceive the culture differently from a new employee who has just been introduced to the company through orientation. The long-term employee will compare the company of the past with the company of the present, while the new employee will only see the company of the present. These views will have some common elements, but much will be different.

Consequently, an organization's culture can only be described by those traits that many or most of the employees perceive. Typically, they are:

- the historical success of the company,
- the legacy of the founders,
- the appeal of its vision and strategy,
- its operational effectiveness,
- its ability to carry out its resolve, and
- its probability of success in the future.

In many ways, culture is the organization's personality. Many authors[10] have attempted to describe the organization's personality, using terms that describe individual, group, and organizational characteristics.

The organizational culture is difficult to change. Like the informal organization component, it mirrors the dysfunction in or among the inner five components. It is a dependent variable, reflecting changes in the other organizational components. Boards of Directors and Executives do not change cultures, they change reporting structures, information systems, technologies, and executive behaviors, all of which in turn change the culture. Because culture is perception, it only changes when what is being perceived changes or the perceiver changes.

For example, executives can change how they conduct meetings—starting on time, following agendas, using a clear set of problem solving tools—and thus change their behavior. Done on a consistent basis over an

---

[10] To start, see:

Willaim Bridges, *The Character of Organizations,* Palo Alto, CA: Consulting Psychologists Press, Inc., 1992.

T. E. Deal and A. A. Kennedy, *Corporate Culture: The Rites and Rituals of Corporate Life,* Reading, MA: Addison-Wesely, 1982.

Joanne Martin, *Culture in Organizations: Three Perspectives,* New York: Oxford University Press, 1992.

Edgar Schein, *Organizational Culture and Leadership,* San Francisco: Jossey-Bass, Inc., 1985.

extended period of time, the perceiver will see this as a significant change in one or two components, and view the culture differently. Or the employee can leave her current employer, work in several different companies that have vastly different cultures, and return to her original company, viewing the company's culture in a much different light.

Like an individual's personality, organizational culture reveals different aspects of itself in different situations to different people. An aggressive, hard-charging company may be viewed as cutthroat by its competitors but as smart and opportunistic by its employees. A large government organization may be viewed by the public as bureaucratic and unresponsive, but viewed by the employees as careful and cautious, acting appropriately in protecting the public's interests.

Chapter Three
Building Your Own Flexible Organization

> "The appearance of reality, according to Mahayana Buddhism, is based upon the interdependence of all things."
>
> Gary Zukav
> *The Dancing Wu Li Masters*

Basics

To design, build, and maintain a flexible organization, executives must follow the basic formula discussed in Chapter I, matching the organizational design to the dynamics of the market. Executives must implement a four step, continually looping process:

1. Align the company's strategy with the marketplace;
2. Align the organizational components with the strategy (inter-component congruence);
3. Ensure congruence of the sub-systems within each component (intra-component congruence);
4. Return to step 1 and begin the process again.

Realigning is a continual process of adjusting and adapting to changes in the markets. The process is usually murky, filled with a mixed bag of information, some clear and some obscure. Experienced executives are keenly aware when their companies are out of alignment, sensing when unseen shifts have occurred. They react by leading and orchestrating corresponding alignment shifts, maintaining organizational balance. They check first for alignment, then balance inter-component and intra-component congruency.

The aligning process is seldom overt or sequential. If it were a phenomenon occurring in the marsh, observers would video tape it, edit it, and show the aligning process as deliberate, purposeful, and sequential. This chapter will use the same approach to organizational alignment process, making overt what is usually covert, and placing intention on actions that are not always intentional.

As a first step in understanding how this works, imagine for a moment that People-Centered Organization® components are the same as information cells on a train board. The process of how the organizational components are interrelated and change simultaneously is similar to the changes in the overhead train boards in any large train station, like Penn Station in New York City or Thirtieth Street Station in Philadelphia.

Table 1 Train Board at 9:00 A.M.

Time	Train #	Train	From	To	Status	Stair
9:10	127	Silver Meteor	New York	Washington	5 min. late	3
9:23	342	Milwaukee Special	New York	Milwaukee	On time	6
9:27	298	Matawan	New Haven	Red Bank	10 min. late	8

As the Silver Meteor leaves, every cell in each of the seven columns on the train board changes to provide a new set of information. Each cell is adjusted to reflect the information about the specific train and is congruent with the train name and train number. Passengers may gain whatever information they may need by glancing at the train board.

Table 2 Train Board at 9:14 A.M.

Time	Train #	Train	From	To	Status	Stair
9:23	342	Milwaukee Special	New York	Milwaukee	5 min. late	Changed to 5
9:27	298	Matawan	New Haven	Red Bank	delayed	will be posted
9:34	671	Trentonian	New York	Trenton	On time	7

Table #2 illustrates the new train information that appears once the Silver Meteor leaves the station, posts any changed or new information about trains previously on the board, and introduces new trains that the board now has space for. In this mechanistic analogy, any new information posted on the board requires corresponding changes throughout the board.

Organizational design is similar. Executives identify where the market is headed, choose a strategy to move the organization to the destination, and then realign the seven components of the People-Centered Organization®. In its simplest form, organizational redesign—creating flexible organizations—is simply aligning the components to the appropriate strategy.

Building further on this analogy to better understand the redesigning process, imagine for a moment that each train is owned and operated by a separate company. Each company has a different niche and a strategy to succeed in the niche. Each company only operates the one train and cannot operate any others. All three companies are profitable and successful by the standards set by their Boards of Directors. Consequently, each train represents the company's entire organization. Conceptual descriptors for organization board for the passenger train industry might look like the table on page 42.

Each train company's alignment and congruency demonstrates how different companies, all in the same industry, can be successful by choosing a niche and clear strategy, aligning the components, and ensuring congruency among and within them.

The Orient Express Company

Market Niche and Strategy

The Orient Express's niche is the high end of the market. Its market is really a resort market and not the transportation market. The Orient Express competes with luxury hotels and resorts for the entertainment dollar of the wealthy. The market is extremely competitive, highly faddish, but steady. The company performs well in all phases of the economic cycle.

Table 3   Train Companies: Alignment of the People-Centered Organization® Components

Market Niche and Strategy	Genetic Core	Philosophy	Formal Organization	Information, Technology, Work Processes	Behavior	Informal Organization	Culture
High end of the luxury train market: Orient Express	Mix of 5 star hotel managers, experienced railroad operators, and luxury car marketers	Provide the highest service and earn the highest margins	Traditional organization structure, control processes focus on guest satisfaction, high performance expectations and tough evaluation; highest wages in industry	Information focuses on always knowing the guest needs and wants, technology provides complete guest history, wants and dislikes	Anticipatory, professional, respectful toward guests; demanding of employees, continual challenging to meet new heights	Elitist and exclusive, long probationary period before belonging, competitive on performance on job	Exclusive and clubby, symbols indicating status, individual judgment valued, professional service mentality
High end of the commuter market; Washington–New York Metroliner	Mix of financially oriented railroaders and experienced marketers	Provide efficient, fast, and comfortable train service with moderate margins	Tightly controlled traditional hierarchy, rigid financial and schedule expectations, competitive wages	Information focuses on operating efficiencies, technology makes fastest scheduling possible	Brisk, professional, efficient	Values workman like performance	Union and management partnership
High end of local commuter market: Princeton Junction to New York.	Financially oriented, tough nosed operators	Move as many commuters as possible faster than major competitors	Lean and mean flattened structure cross-functional jobs, evaluated on financial results	Information and technology focus on maximizing customer per square foot ratio, work processes are rigid and strictly adhered to, to ensure safety and best cost utilization	Commodity business means that we treat each other and customers like a commodity	Stratified by rank and job category	Pervasive get the job done, work your eight hours and enjoy something else

Genetic Core

The Board of Directors guides the company with an approach matched to its niche. The executives in the genetic core have been recruited into the organization for their particular backgrounds and experiences. The strategy in developing the genetic core was to mix knowledge and expertise from different service industry companies that provide five star service to create a team that is greater than the sum of its parts. The team should be able to blend individual backgrounds and knowledge, taking the best from each to form an executive brain trust capable of creating a rolling luxury hotel that everyone wants to ride.

Philosophy

The corporate philosophy is direct and clear: we are the best of the best. The strategy of the philosophy component is to embed a customer service ethic as the preeminent value in the organization's and the employees' daily life. Decisions at all levels and types, strategic and tactical, are made using this as a criteria. This living philosophy demonstrates to all stakeholders that the corporation strives to be uniquely superior.

Formal Organization

The formal organization is traditional. The genetic core manages the corporation with a firm and benevolent hand that continually guides the organization to providing superior service. The control systems track performance to ensure high standards with little margin for error. Policy and procedures emphasize that employees will be well rewarded for meeting company goals and quickly dismissed if management feels they are not able to perform to expectations. Wages are the best in the industry, matching the expectations of individual performance. The evaluation process is from the top down and based on team performance in meeting customer service and profit margin goals.

Information, Technology, and Work Processes

The company's strategy for the information and technology systems is to use them as competitive advantages. The company maintains state of the art information systems to be able to provide higher quality, quicker, more efficient service than its competitors. All railroad functions have the same on-line, real time access to data. The information system is designed to provide comprehensive detail on guests' needs to any employee that needs it. Employees can access the data bases from the train, determining a guest's destination, dining preferences, or future booked excursions. Similarly, the maintenance repair shop has the capability to call up a total data base on any piece of equipment owned by the company.

The work processes strategy is the same. It is designed to provide superior service. They are annually reviewed by a special task force, a group of superior performers, who review and alter them as needed to ensure highest quality service. All employees are required to strictly follow the redesigned work processes, and all suggestions for improvement must go through a rigorous approval process prior to being considered by the special task force.

Behavior

To ensure that all employees treat guests with the greatest respect and dignity, the strategy for the behavior component is to treat everyone, guests and fellow employees, as if they were a guest. The company emphasizes politeness, precise communication, timely completion of tasks, and complete follow through. It provides training programs on respectful behavior, meeting internal customer needs, and surpassing guests' expectations. Meetings are crisp and timely. Agendas are required for all meetings, facilitators are appointed whenever necessary, and clear decision making rules are enforced.

Informal Organization

The informal organization's strategy is to create a sense of exclusivity. Prior to being accepted as a member of the informal organization, employees must prove themselves to their peers by their performance. The informal organization excludes new employees, forcing them to perform their roles with little or no support from peers until their character and ability have been thoroughly judged. Once they are accepted, employees live in a protective cocoon which reinforces their membership in the exclusive club. Peers will assist in guiding their careers, help correct mistakes, and collaborate on ways to improve service to guests and internal customers.

Culture

The strategy of the culture component is to reinforce the exclusive nature and the exacting standards of the Orient Express. The employee lounge on board rivals any of the exclusive guest compartments and the employee menu is always the same as the guest menu. Uniform insignia indicate rank and years of service. Achievement awards are difficult to earn, well publicized within the company, and valued highly by most employees. Management holds lavish company functions to confer special status and privilege to high performers. The annual events are held in prestigious hotels, and expensive gifts are awarded to the honorees.

The Metroliner Company

Market Niche and Strategy

The New York-Washington Metroliner company's market is also a high end market but totally different from the Orient Express's market. The Metroliner market is several million harried business people who need to travel between the major cities on the East Coast. They need the speed and convenience of the normal commuter train and can afford a few extra amenities. The market is extremely competitive, leaving little room for error. The Metroliner competes with the local commuter trains, buses, short hop airlines, and the personally-owned automobile.

To be successful in this market, the Metroliner company must develop a competitive advantage in four variables: time, price, value, and convenience. The train must be faster than the commuter trains, cheaper than the airlines while still close in price to the commuter trains, and provide more service and comfort than a commuter train, bus, or car. Additionally, it must be easy for passengers to access and must deliver them to high density business locales. However, these competitive advantages are unobtainable because they are mutually exclusive qualities. Easy access is impossible from high density business locations, and consequently the train company is forced to emphasize speed, price, and value.

The business strategy is to always be 15% faster than the fastest commuter train, never greater than 50% more expensive than the commuter train, and always 50% less costly than the airline short hop. Additionally, the train buys and maintains equipment that is more comfortable than the commuter train, and offers limited dining services. It must provide more reliable service than the commuter train, and avoid being hindered by weather like the airline short hops. In short, the strategy is to provide more value and reliability than its competitors.

Genetic Core

The Metroliner Company's strategy for the genetic core is to assemble an executive team that understands the incessant demands of providing commuter service with the skills of promoting a service in a very competitive market. The genetic core consists of executives from operations and marketing backgrounds. The operational executives are experienced commuter railroad managers who know how to operate an efficient and profitable train. They have proven expertise in managing track, equipment and people. The marketing core members come from the financial services, where service and products are not highly differentiated and marketing is frequently the only competitive advantage. The management team members are also screened for flexibility, with proven past ability to change tactics and strategies in response to new competition.

Philosophy

The Company philosophy's strategy is to encourage smooth, efficient operations that maximize investment. The philosophy states that the company intends "to provide the best possible value in commuting between major East Coast cities, maximizing each and every opportunity to provide efficient service to the customer." The philosophy further states that "management and employees recognize the highly competitive nature of the industry, and understand that every one must contribute to the company's profitability." Clearly, the Company wants to impress on its employees that lean and mean is the only way for the company to survive.

Formal Organization

The formal organization's strategy is to create structure and processes that allow employees to use their best judgment in operating the trains on time and as fully loaded as possible. Consequently, the train conductor will hold a train past scheduled departure, waiting for late arriving reservation holders. The engineer and the division head then work together to determine where and when the train can make up the lost time. To help create this type of goal-oriented working relationships, the hierarchy is flat. The reporting relationships are clear, but employees understand that there are no functional or personal empires. Employees are rewarded on team goals, and individual evaluations are cross-functional, done by internal customers.

Paradoxically, the control processes are fixed by upper management and are used to control operations tightly. The strategy is to create a strong framework of processes that counterbalance and reinforce the flattened hierarchy, keeping everyone focused on meeting goals. Operating functions must meet their financial goals and predetermined strategy seldom changes. Career movement is limited. Once an employee proves that she is competent, she is required to continuously improve, but not encouraged to move to another position.

The reward system is congruent with the philosophy. Wages are competitive, fluctuating as needed with the market. Employees know and understand that the company emphasizes value, and that management views wages as performance driven. Teams are typically recognized for outstanding performance rather than individuals, although exceptional individual performances are acknowledged and rewarded.

Information, Technology, and Work Processes

The strategy of the information, technology, and work processes component is to provide decision makers with information that highlights trends that make the train successful. Additional detail to the trends is available and readily accessible by those in the need. The information component's purpose, like the railroad's operating philosophy, is to provide only what will be used and valued.

Technology is the key to the Metroliner company's success. Identifying, obtaining, operating, and maintaining high-quality, durable, efficient equipment is a major factor in the railroad's success. The technological strategy is to purchase and operate the most durable equipment, maximizing its life by providing outstanding maintenance. Management again views this simply as an extension of the company's philosophy, maximizing value in a capital-investment-laden business.

The strategy for the work processes is paradoxical, like the control processes in the formal organization. The work processes are time honored, proven ways to operate a railroad. Management expects employees to follow procedures, and then use individual judgment. If a work process interferes with on-time arrival, and no safety violation is involved, employees are encouraged to use their own judgment to find the best way to maximize volume or stay on schedule.

Behavior

The strategy for the behavior component is to emphasize that every employee is a professional within his or her own area of expertise, and within the railroading industry. Each employee is treated like a professional who has ideas to contribute, a perspective to share, and is interested in helping the company solve problems. Decisions are discussed but not debated, and participation is limited to an employee's area of expertise. Employees are kept informed of the company's financial and key operating statistics. Management, consistent with the reward system, stresses team work and the contribution of all the teams to the success of the company.

Informal Organization

The informal organization supports the company while maintaining a healthy skepticism. The employees are unionized and the informal organization encourages participation in union activities. The union is viewed by its leaders as a safety net to be used in the event that management changes significantly or some other factor forces a change in operating philosophy or strategy. As a union shop, employees are welcomed as dues paying members, educated in past management fiascoes, and informed that the current management acts as if they know what they are doing. Cooperation with management is encouraged and the successes of the past ten years are shared. The informal organization views itself as a partner with the formal organization, a partnership that is currently successful and that will continue to work well if both sides work together.

Culture

The strategy for the organizational culture is to emphasize the value of teamwork and current success. Consequently, both union and management place symbols of successful cooperation throughout the company. The employee lounge's and corporate headquarters' walls are covered with company, team, and individual achievement awards. Plaques commemorating union-management agreements and memorable moments in the company cover the walls. Annual giveaways, hats, cups, jackets, sponsored by both the union and the company, are distributed to everyone. Perhaps most importantly, employees and management act as if the partnership works on a daily basis.

The Daily Commuter Company

Market Niche and Strategy

The Daily Commuter Company is in the toughest business in the industry, hauling commuters from one point to another, at the low end of the market. The company's business strategy is dictated by its market: move as many passengers per square foot of equipment and per mile of track as possible. To successfully compete in the mass transit market, the Daily Commuter Company must think like a warehouse company, that is, maximize use of available space. The business strategy, as passed along on the grapevine, is "to squeeze everything and everybody to max."

The Company's competition is plentiful. The Company competes against the local businesses that shuttle passengers quickly to New York, cars that provide the driver with flexibility in the commute to New York, and other commuter trains that originate in nearby towns. The only competitive advantage that The Daily Commuter has is its reputation for reliability. The company cannot compete on price because the market is so competitive that prices are already as low as possible. The Company cannot compete on value because the only valued service is reliable service. Consistency, steadfastness, and durability are the key qualities in the battle to win customers and remain profitable.

The Daily Commuter strategy is to blend reliable service and financial shrewdness. The company must leverage its capital investment to keep costs at a minimum. It must also maintain competitive prices not only with its commuting train competitors, but minimize the attractiveness of the convenience of the bus and the flexibility of the automobile. Additionally, the Company must operate a robust schedule that offers as many commuting times as possible, again, to compete with the buses and automobiles. Consequently, the strategy of "squeeze everything and everybody to max," makes a great deal of business sense.

Genetic Core

The Company's genetic core is filled with executives experienced in the railroad commuting industry. The Board of Directors' strategy for the genetic core is to fill it with executives who have extensive expertise operating an efficient and reliable railroad. The genetic core, like the Company, is a group that is a no frills, focus on the business personality. The genetic core members all have operating backgrounds and all a long record of financial conservatism. All of the Company's key functions— Operations, Finance, Marketing and Sales, Maintenance and Safety—are headed by executives who have had direct operating experience. Managers with functional expertise, such as marketing and finance, are the next level down in the organization.

Philosophy

The Daily Commuter's philosophy is "We are the toughest in a tough industry." The Company's strategy for the philosophy is to set guidelines that create an environment fostering a hard-nosed work ethic, and a sense of personal responsibility for the capital assets of the Company. The philosophy identifies two core values that describe the type of people the Company hires and the way they should behave: (1) getting the job done in all conditions, and (2) doing the job better than anyone else.

Formal Organization

The formal organization's strategy is simplicity. The organization's structure is lean and mean, even more than other commuter companies. The Company has four major functional areas with direct-line reporting relationships. Cross-functional work is usually done by the functional head or assistant head. The Company has three tiers of management, function head, function assistant, and manager. Non-managerial employees are unionized and promoted according to seniority and performance. Wages are competitive with a gain-sharing program that is tied to year-end profitability.

The control systems are managed top down. Input from functional and departmental managers is solicited by formal request, and typically restricted to the top levels of management. Strategic business plans are developed for each department and become the roadmap for the year.

Every process is carefully measured and monitored. Management expects everyone to strictly adhere to their prescribed budgets and operating ratios. For example, operating equipment has a projected lifetime with specified maintenance. Each unit of rolling stock receives a predetermined amount of maintenance based on operating experience. Any additional maintenance to a rolling stock must be explained to head of maintenance, including what the extra maintenance was and why it was needed.

Employees are evaluated by their supervisors on a bi-annual basis. Consistent with the philosophy, the evaluations are short and to the point. Performance expectations are clear and the employees are expected to meet all previously set goals. The union and management have negotiated minimum performance standards and if the employee fails to meet the minimum, he or she is immediately released. Significant mistakes are recorded in the employee's file and more than three in a year is cause for discharge.

Information, Technology, and Work Processes

The strategy of the information, technology, and work processes is to support the railroad's durability. All three systems are designed and maintained to keep the people, equipment, and work flow going no matter what the conditions. The information system provides employees and management with on-time performance measures, equipment status, employee availability status, and financial performance. The operating technology, the railroad equipment, is purchased for its ruggedness and durability. Equipment is purchased only after it has proven its durability on other commuter lines in harsher climates. Congruent with its durability strategy, management purchases maintenance equipment on a state of the art basis. The Company buys the best and most advanced maintenance equipment to maximize its investment in its rolling stock and other capital equipment.

The work processes are time-tested, trusted, proven ways of accomplishing repetitive tasks. Management has documented the processes, and updates them annually based on new equipment purchases, safety regulations, and technological changes. Any other changes in the work processes must be approved by a joint union and Company task force.

Behavior

The strategy for the behavior component is to focus the employees on getting the job done. Employees treat each other as busy people who have important jobs to be done. Communication is typically focused on the problem or issue at hand. Decisions are made using well-established problem-solving processes. Meeting participants must do their homework, distributing completed analyses prior to any decision-making meetings. Meetings are short, having two major purposes, problem-solving or communication sharing. Managers direct, employees follow. Managers decide, employees recommend.

Informal Organization

The Company's informal organization counterbalances the grim professionalism of the other components. The informal organization is the Company's network for having fun. It is full of sports teams, social groups, trips, and employee benefit activities. The network assistance ranges from helping an employee with a quick tutoring lesson on how to succeed in a particular job, to where to find the lowest rates for a personal loan.

Culture

The strategy for the Company's culture is to emphasize the time honored ethos of hard work and proven methods. Management stresses understanding the company's competitive environment and following proven ways to succeed "in the toughest business." The union and the Company both reward longevity as an acknowledgment that an individual is tough, knowledgeable, and reliable. The symbols for longevity, reliability, and frugality abound. The corporate headquarters is in a Spartan, drab building near the New Jersey terminus. When you enter the lobby the first artifact you see is a 95-year-old turnstile prominently displayed. It is one of the first that the Company purchased.

The informal organization also acts as an impromptu recruiting and temporary help agency. The Company hires through the informal network, taking the suggestions from employees of who would make a good employee. Current employees keep in contact with former employees who wish to work part time or who are available in an emergency replacement situation.

Summary

Each of these three hypothetical companies, The Orient Express, The Metroliner Company, and The Daily Commuter illustrate several key points:

❏ well-designed organizations have their organizational components strategically aligned, congruent with each other;
❏ intra-component congruency is just as important as inter-component congruency; and
❏ strategic alignment and component congruency are relatively easy to create in a stable market.

The three railroad companies demonstrate how executives can create organizations that are strategically aligned to the dynamics of their markets. The examples assume that the markets are stable and well understood. Understanding their markets, the executives developed strategies that exploited a particular niche, and designed an organization that created and maintained core competencies and capabilities to continue to exploit the niche.

The interlocking, reinforcing nature of the congruent organizational components ensured that the company's employees live and behave within a strategic organizational framework or envelope. Because the companies are strategically aligned, and because congruency creates a clear path to success, the employees have a well-defined world to work in. The strategic intent of each company was embedded in every aspect of every component. The way to success was well documented and well defined.

The inter-component congruency—the congruency between what the Daily Commuter expects of its employees and how it pays them—is the second step in the rebalancing process. The third step is intra-component congruency. The congruency between the Metroliner Company's work processes and the information available to make the decisions required by the work processes is as important as inter-component congruency. Companies must have both to be highly successful. The final step is to return to aligning, determining if the strategy still matches the market.

The strategic alignment and congruency principles are even more important in unstable or rapidly changing markets. In the three railroad companies, the strategic alignment and congruency principles reinforce each other and create a strategic, living framework to guide employees. However, in rapidly changing markets, strategic alignment will be continually adjusting and responding to the market. Component congruency will be in a constant state of flux, as the strategic alignment shifts create corresponding changes in the inter- and intra-component congruency.

Section II
Viewing an Inflexible
and a Flexible Organization

"Example is the school of mankind, and they will learn at no other."

Edmund Burke
Letters on a Regicide Peace

Introduction

Chapters One through Three discussed how organizations work, introduced People-Centered Organizations® framework to view organizations, and depicted the concepts in detail in three hypothetical railroad companies. Section Two, Chapters Four and Five, illustrate how organizations work when viewed through the People-Centered Organizations® approach. Both case studies in this Section are actual organizations. Their descriptions are altered only to protect the confidentiality of the two companies.

Chapter 4
How Organizational Inflexibility Creates Dysfunction

"In rigid families the passage from one evolutionary stage to the next may be perceived as catastrophic. The necessity for change becomes transmuted into the adopting of a known solution, applied in the present and 'programmed' for the future. The family is closed to any experimentation and new learning. A solution which had served in one phase is rigidly applied in others."

> Maurizo Andolfi, Claudio Angelo,
> Paolo Menghi, and Anna Maria
> Nicolo-Corigliano
> *Behind the Family Mask*

Overview

Inflexible organizations cannot respond quickly to external changes, shifts in market dynamics or labor pool demographics. Nor can they respond to internal changes, such as new technological capabilities or process improvements. Inflexible organizations become rigid because of the biological and psychological principle of homeostasis,[11][12] the tendency of any system to seek the balance it had prior to any action interrupting it. Calm pond water, disturbed by a single stone thrown into it, will return to its calmness, if no further stones are thrown. The water seeks to return to its previous state, returning to its initial homeostasis. If, however, the stones are piled to create a dam, the water must adjust to the permanent alteration. The dam creates an imbalance in the pond that

---

[11] James Miller. ibid.

[12] Kurt Lewin, *Field Theory in Social Science,* New York: Harper and Row Publishers, 1951.

the former equilibrium does not fit, and consequently the system seeks a new balance.

Inflexible organizations are caught in a rigid imbalance because they are always returning to the initial homeostasis. External and internal changes seem to make no difference to the organization. Once the stone has been thrown, the shock waves ripple throughout the organization, but make no permanent change. Rigid organizations fail to shift to a new strategic alignment or a new congruence, because the change is not powerful enough to break the current homeostasis. Inflexible organizations are locked into their present organizational design and are unable to shift to a new design.

Executives create inflexible organizations by failing to apply the five basic principles governing organizations. Inflexible organizations fail and become dysfunctional because they:

❑   are not in strategic alignment, or
❑   do not have inter-component or intra-component congruency, or
❑   act as if one component of the company is not interdependent with the others, or
❑   do not understand that people are the organization, or
❑   have a high degree of any of the above

Why do these failures create inflexibility and rigidity? Because inflexible organizations send contradictory and conflicting messages to their employees. Unlike the railroad companies which were strategically aligned and congruent, inflexible companies send mixed messages about their direction, purpose, and strategic intent. If the Orient Express Company kept its stated strategy of providing luxury entertainment but flooded employees with information like the Daily Commuter on how to maximize profit per square foot, then the employees would receive contradictory and conflicting messages.

On receiving the contradictory messages, individuals can make one of four choices:

❑   act in accordance with a strategy that they believe will be in the best interest of the company,

- ❑ act in accordance with a strategy that they believe will be in the best interest of their function or their boss,
- ❑ act in accordance with a strategy that meets their own best interest, or
- ❑ do nothing because they do not want be wrong or be blamed.

Only the first choice has a chance of being productive for the company. Choosing any one of the other three options is simply acting in one's perceived best interest, without any guidance as to what might be most beneficial to the company.

The dilemma for both the organization and the company is that acting in one's best interest is critical to good mental health. Most individuals are healthier mentally when they choose actions that help them achieve their goals, that are consistent with their values, and that have at least a minimum congruence with the group they live in. In other words, individuals need to choose how they will behave based on their needs and the dynamics of their environments. (There is more on this in Chapter Six.) Without clear direction from the company or in the face of contradictory and conflicting messages of how to act in the company's best interest, individuals choose to act in their self-interest.

Consequently, inflexible organizations have their people acting in their own best interests, unable or unwilling to work together, and frequently working against each other. Without a clearer goal stating the greater self-interest, some employees cluster into functional fiefdoms or small groups, avoiding the impact of other stronger and more powerful groups. Other employees seek refuge in cynicism and rage, refusing to connect with any group until the organization is able to heal itself.

Inflexible organizations become rigid as they are pushed into a dysfunctional homeostasis by lack of a strategic alignment and incongruency. Caught in a vicious cycle, the dysfunctional homeostasis is particularly powerful because it is continually reinforced by the contradictory messages on three levels: organization, team, and individual. Everyone in the organization becomes comfortable with the dysfunction, and the dysfunction becomes the norm, the new homeostasis.

The Case of the Orphaned Company

Background

Dysfunctional companies, rigidly caught in their own pathology are unable to break the dysfunctional patterns that trap them in failure. The SCC company is a perfect example of a company that trapped its employees in a conflicting and incongruent system.

The SCC[13] Company is a manufacturer of specialty coatings for industrial purposes. SCC was created twenty-five years ago by two research chemists who developed a formula for specialty coatings. Although they clearly saw that their coatings could be a profitable product line, the executives of their Fortune 500 Company Division did not believe that the market was large enough to justify further expenditures on the coatings. The research chemists were encouraged to take their formula and create their own company.

Like many other corporate sagas of this type, the research chemists left the Fortune 500 Company, formed their own company, and became immensely successful. Within five years, they developed a company that grossed 10 million dollars in sales and generated twenty-five percent margins. Their coatings proved to be innovative and greatly superior to any competitor's product. Remaining true to their research background, the research chemists continued to develop new formulas and applications. SCC's profits allowed them to experiment and create as much as they liked.

Not surprisingly, larger companies, looking to branch into new markets, purchase a small cash cow, or both, were soon interested in acquiring SCC. The research chemists received purchase offers that would make them millionaires, allow them to stay with the company, and free them from some of the burden of managing the company so that they could continue their research. Like most researchers, the promise of freedom from the demands of management, and the opportunity to become independently wealthy, tempted them to sell SCC. So, they sold the company to a Fortune 100 corporation, invested their money, and managed the company as a subsidiary.

The research chemists soon found that managing the company with the help of the parent company was a greater burden than managing it

---

[13] Although SCC is a fictitious name, the company is real. All names have been changed to protect the company's and the individuals' privacy.

alone. As soon as the Fortune 100 company imposed its systems on SCC, professionalizing management practices, and standardizing systems, one of the research chemists retired from the company. The other remained as CEO, but eventually stepped aside for an executive from the parent company, remaining as director of R&D. He was never pleased with how the new CEO was running the company, and spent much of his time influencing managers and employees to follow his management approach rather than the CEOs. The resulting schism hurt profitability and volume, causing the parent company to rethink its ownership position.

Before long, the parent company decided to sell SCC, having found that selling SCC would be more profitable than operating it. The parent company found another Fortune 500 company looking to enter the coatings market and desiring a small cash cow to build into a major force in the market. SCC was sold, the remaining research chemist retired, and SCC was now positioned to become a significant acquisition for its second parent company.

SCC never did become a major acquisition for the second Fortune 500 owner nor for the next six corporate owners over the next ten years. In fact, SCC became a corporate orphan, bought and sold eight times in a fifteen year period. Each time it was purchased by a major corporation, the intent was always the same. SCC's knowledge of coatings and its strong R&D capabilities, combined with good management, would catapult SCC into a major force in the market. Each time the promise lasted anywhere from twelve months to three years, then SCC was sold to another corporation.

Market Niche and Strategy

When the research chemists created SCC, they immediately jumped in front of their competitors. SCC's coatings were state of the art, able to out perform any other coating on the market. The chemists were delighted to discover how quickly their coatings were accepted in the market. Sales were so strong that they did not need a sales staff. The demand reinforced their bias that good products sold themselves and sales people were needed for companies with inferior products.

Throughout their tenure as owners and managers, SCC's strategy was to maintain its competitive advantage by developing new and superior coatings. The R&D function was the strength of the company, well funded and well staffed. The company's success reinforced the strategy, and generations of executives continued to fund R&D and ignore the sales function.

While the research chemists were involved in the company, R&D thrived. When the second chemist left SCC, the R&D department lost its creative genius. Meanwhile, the competition had narrowed the gap between their coatings and SCC's. The growth of the competition moved the market from an entrepreneurial stage to a growth stage. Service and delivery time became key competitive advantages of the market in the growth stage. Despite the changes, SCC's management still believed that developing new products was a strategy for success.

SCC tried to pursue its R&D strategy without its resident genius in the newly competitive market. At first, the absentee corporate owners installed competent managers, but poor strategists. They assumed that SCC simply needed professional management to continue providing healthy profits. Although SCC continued to be very profitable, it stopped growing. Competitors cut into its market share by beating SCC on service and delivery time. As the market became even more competitive, moving into a mature stage, cost became a key advantage. SCC was unable to compete on cost, because of its expensive strategy to invest heavily in R&D.

Eventually one of the parent companies hired an executive who was a proven strategist. He emphasized sales, hiring a market and sales executive, identified target markets, and installed a formal strategic planning process. But he did not reduce R&D expenditures, and in several markets, decided to use unproved new products in several markets. Neither his target marketing nor his new product strategy was successful and he was soon replaced by a manufacturing-oriented executive who continued his strategy!

Why was SCC never able to fulfill its promise? The answers, according to two sets of its corporate owners, two CEOs, several generations of managers, and numerous long-term employees are:

❑   the parent company was always squeezing it for too much cash;
❑   the CEOs were incompetent as strategists, marketers, motivators, and leaders (pick one or more);
❑   the employees were unwilling to work together;
❑   the product was never as good as its reputation;
❑   no one knew how to apply the product in a cost efficient way;

❑   the sales force was inadequate and unable to sell a great product; and

❑   SCC always lost is best employees to its competitors.

Unfortunately, the respondents are all correct. SCC, launched by two entrepreneurs, became stuck in its original strategic alignment and congruency. Over the years, it failed to change to meet new market dynamics, and the demands of new owners. The root cause of SCC's failure was its failure to change as a whole system.

Genetic Core

The research chemists were brilliant as research chemists, but not so brilliant as managers. They were good entrepreneurs, but poor manufacturing specialists. They were innovative in developing new applications, but poor in selling the idea to the market. In short, they were exactly what they trained to be and aspired to be. They left SCC with a typical entrepreneurial legacy—brilliant product capabilities and poor management, a genetic imprint that has haunted SCC ever since.

More specifically, SCC's legacy from the original genetic core was a proud innovator, an arrogant manufacturer, a spurner of sales efforts, and a spinner of intrigue. When the research chemists founded the company, their product was so superior that it sold itself. More accurately, the chemists had more than enough customers for their tiny company to serve. Like entrepreneurs all over the world, they hired a few dedicated employees who enjoyed making a new product, being the first to do something new, and passionately believing in the superiority of their product.

The original employees and the research chemists developed into a family group, becoming very close to each other, knowing everything that happened to each other, and understanding exactly what each other would do without ever being told.

They did not need to formalize relationships, systems, or communication. They had no formal meetings, simply sitting down to coffee together was sufficient. This simple and powerful organizational design worked well for them during SCC's entrepreneurial stage.

When they sat together to have coffee, they discussed which customers they would like to keep and which they were not interested in. They would sometimes discuss how to improve working together, but it

Table 4   SCC at a Glance

Market	Strategy	Genetic Core	Philosophy	Formal Organization	Information, Technology, Work Processes	Behavior	Informal Organization	Culture
Niche: Specialty coatings for industry	Develop new and superior products that sell themselves.	Heavily biased to research and new product development.	We know best, the customer knows very little.	Traditional hierarchy, with strong department identity and independence.	Information used as a political weapon.	Behavior inconsistent with verbal communication.	Close knit, vicious, nasty, and destructive.	Negative self-image disguised behind arrogance.
Market Stage: When the company was founded, the market was in a start-up stage. At the time of the writing, the market was in a mature stage, with many competitors.		Strong emphasis on denial—believing that no sales force was needed, and that no competitor could make a product as well as SCC. Strong rebellious attitude against professional management and big corporations.	We have the best technology.	R&D is the most powerful of all functions, followed by manufacturing. Reward system designed to match corporate owners' needs, not market. Evaluation system used sporadically and used to reinforce department loyalty.	Technology poorly understood and used. Few formal work process- manufacturing is an art form.	Most issues and problems were left to fester.	Also very protective of its long time members. Rejects new members. Keeps members frozen in well known behavioral patterns, prevents change.	Insullar and remote from outside world.

was more natural and therefore easier, to discuss how to make the product better. As long as they kept improving the product, they continued to have a core of customers that was more than enough to increase sales and generate high margins.

When they needed to add more employees, the research chemists asked current employees to find potential new employees. Consequently, friends and neighbors of the current employees were added to the work force. SCC was too small to have a new employee orientation program, and the new employees learned how SCC worked through on the job training.

The on the job training process was effective, but ultimately dysfunctional. The new employees were quickly assimilated into the "just get it done culture" and learned to admire the product and the company's technological capabilities. They learned to like the informality and the camaraderie. Of course, they were predisposed to like SCC because their friends liked SCC.

The new employees did learn to function well in a chaotic, but still relatively successful organization. They soon learned who to see on a particular issue and enjoyed SCC's sense of family. Unfortunately, they also learned they knew better than the customer, for only they really understood the capabilities of the product. They learned the product was so good that most customers sought them out, and they learned that customers will wait to buy a superior product. When the company was first sold, they learned that the company could still survive despite the CEO and some of the managers going in one direction, and the research chemist and other managers and employees going in another. They learned how to survive in a company that was no longer congruent.

Another legacy was built into the genetic core from the addition of new employees from the local area. The company was located in a rural area, dominated by farmers and only a few small companies. The local population was ruggedly independent in spirit, wary of big companies and employees of big companies. They were accustomed to solving problems by themselves, then announcing the solution to their peers. They perceived small as good, and large as bad. They believed that country people were inherently smarter and better than city people, and that city people were not to be trusted.

Consequently, when SCC was sold the first time, the managers and employees were pleased for their friends, the research chemists, but leery of being managed by executives who were both from a big company and a big city. As the first corporate owner tried to impose new systems on SCC, the employees did not see the need, and being naturally suspicious of big corporations, resisted. As the parent company persisted in implementing new systems, the employees' discomfort increased. They appealed to the research chemist to help them avoid the impositions that the new systems placed on everyone. Naturally, the research chemist supported his employees, and began to actively resist the parent company's intentions. The final piece of the SCC genetic core legacy was set. A small, dedicated group of employees had the original owner's blessing to resist the parent company's efforts to bring about change, no matter what the benefits of the change might be.

Philosophy

SCC's original philosophy, most likely unspoken, was to produce a unique product, generating high margins to fund further applied research. Customers were viewed as an unfortunate, yet necessary part of doing business. SCC, like most other companies in the 1950's, paid little or no attention to customer service. But even more than its contemporaries, it perfected the art of keeping the customer from getting in the way. Customers were a necessary evil who did not understand their equipment or the equipment's problems. Customer complaints and service problems were simply customers not understanding SCC. Regardless of how they were treated, customers always returned to SCC because the product was superior.

Over the years, the philosophy did not change as the company and the market changed. When the last of the two original owners retired, the R&D function lost much of its creative force. Over the years, SCC did not significantly improve its products. Many of its competitors copied its technology, leaving SCC with only its reputation as a competitive advantage. Despite the changes in the market, the company, the product (or lack of product changes), and SCC's philosophy remained the same. Most of the employees still chose to believe that SCC was a technological leader and could behave like one. SCC's philosophy, like its products and technology, remained rigidly stuck in the past.

Formal Organization

Initially, like all entrepreneurial companies, SCC was a small group of employees working together with little concern for role, position, and education. As the company grew, the research chemists structured the company into traditional functions—manufacturing, accounting, and customer orders. Functional boundaries and responsibilities were blurred because of the small number of employees, the newness of the organization, and need for everyone to wear multiple hats.

However, once SCC was acquired, additional functions were added. One of the early parent companies was able to add two additional functions, engineering and sales, to SCC's structure. The core employee group readily accepted engineering because it was simply an extension of the group drinking coffee, discussing new product applications and derivations, and costing alternatives. Sales however, did not fit into SCC's philosophy. The employees expected Sales to easily locate awe-stricken customers who could hardly wait to use SCC products and services.

By 1993, SCC had six functions: Manufacturing, Accounting, Coating Engineering/Estimates, Specialty Engineering/Estimates, R&D, and Marketing and Sales. A manager headed each function who reported to the CEO. The marketing and sales manager position was vacant. The incumbent had just been released during the most recent downsizing and for the fourth time in three years, the management team was debating whether SCC needed to have a manager for the Marketing and Sales function.

Over the years, SCC's reward system changed as its various corporate owners changed. The 1993 corporate owner was a highly-leveraged holding company, whose major objective in purchasing SCC was for its contribution to cash flow. Consequently, SCC's reward system for managers and employees was linked to cash flow goals. Managers were salaried and employees were paid on a hourly basis, with time and half for over time. Bonuses were based on meeting SCC's cash contribution goals only. Minimal bonuses were paid if SCC met 80% of its IBIT (income before interest and taxes) goals and maximum bonuses paid if 100% of IBIT was met.

SCC's evaluation system was traditional, managers evaluating employees on an annual basis. Executives and managers seldom insisted on completion of the annual evaluations, and several employees and managers often were not evaluated for several years. Annual raises were loosely connected with annual evaluations, depending on the year, the corporate owner, the CEO, and the employee's manager. The quality of customer service and the product were never an integral aspect of the evaluation system. Managers, at the year end meeting to determine salary increases, engaged in a zero sum argument of whose employees would receive the better raise.

SCC's management team seldom acknowledged special contributions or outstanding performance. Only those CEOs, who were able communicators and motivators, would be sure to praise individual effort. Managers only rewarded those employees who loyally supported their functions. Employees were openly encouraged not to cooperate with other departments. In fact, several employees were dismissed over the years for too vigorously pursuing cross-functional teamwork.

Information, Technology, and Work Processes

Information was power in SCC, and typically used as a political weapon against other employees in other functions. Each function kept its own data base of customers, contacts, and other data. In 1993, SCC's midsize computer (an IBM 34) was managed in the accounting function and used for financial records only. Invoices, work orders, and other cross-functional information had to be processed and reconciled by hand. Not surprisingly, the management team never considered expanding SCC's IT capability across functional boundaries as a priority. Manufacturing and R&D usually received the majority of the capital budget, with periodic, panic spending on sales campaigns to revive sagging backlog. Like many other companies, the situation only grew worse when managers started buying personal computers, developing their own data bases and tracking their own departmental costs.

SCC's manufacturing process was considered an art, a form of craftsmanship that required intensive hand labor and years of apprenticeship to learn. Technology was an indispensable part of the manufacturing process, but never perceived as something that could be managed and controlled. For example, a fire destroyed a curing oven in 1992 and SCC had to purchase a new one. The new oven, installed by the manufacturer, soon became an enigma. The manufacturing manager had expected quality to improve with the new oven, but it declined, requiring more rework than ever. The manufacturing supervisory team was puzzled and did not know what the problem was. The oven temperature seemed to be fine, always reading within the right range. Finally, an enterprising employee placed temperature gauges in different locations throughout the oven. He discovered that temperatures varied widely from one location in the oven to another. After the problem was resolved by the oven's manufacturer, quality returned to its normal levels.

SCC did not have any formal work processes. Many repetitive, well-known processes were done differently for different customers, different products, and different times in the month. Work processes varied depending upon the pressure of the moment—an angry customer, a new product, or a demand for bookings in a slow month. New employees modified work processes as they saw best, often receiving little or no support from more experienced peers. If the process worked well, no one commented; if it worked poorly, peers chastised the new employee. A two-year investment in TQM, manifested in task forces trying to improve work processes, stopped after the TQM/QC manager was reassigned to the manufacturing floor during a downsizing.

Behavior

Most of SCC's employees' behavior was passive-aggressive; they said one thing and did another. Individuals promised to cooperate, to share information and responsibility, but never did. Conflict was always lingering below the surface of conversations, but managers and employees never attempted to resolve it. Weekly management meetings were typical of this problem. The meeting was typically chaired by either the CEO or the ranking manager in his absence. Each manager reported on the status of his or her department, always stressing what was completed, what had been achieved, and then adding that any unfinished assignments or major problems were another function's fault.

True to the genetic core legacy, Marketing and Sales became everyone's favorite department to blame. At meeting after meeting, the managers reported on the status of work in their departments. Each week the discussion was the same. Manufacturing was in good shape except that there was not enough volume. Accounting had closed the month except for the outstanding sales expense reports that were overdue. Coating Engineering/Estimates had generated a huge quantity of bids, but marketing and sales had not developed the marketing material to accompany the bids. Specialty Engineering/Estimates was succeeding despite any effort from the marketing and sales department. Finally, the CEO would ask the Marketing and Sales manager what the problem was and he would blame the other departments for not cooperating with his department. The CEO then would privately meet with the Marketing and Sales manager to discuss the problems within his department.

Although most anger was overtly expressed, employee meetings followed the same pattern. Employees would take turns blaming other departments, then argue about who was right and wrong. The only subject that employees could agree upon was how they felt about management. Everyone agreed that management was incompetent, and that the parent company was the source of all evil. During the TQM effort, most problem-solving meetings deteriorated into blaming sessions unless an outside facilitator ran the meeting and forcefully guided the discussion.

SCC employees were loyal to themselves first, their department second, the company third, the customer fourth, and the parent company fifth. Whenever a key decision had to be made, employees decided what was best for themselves, then the department. If a choice had to be made between what was best for the department or the company, the department won. If the choice was between what was best for the company or the customer, the company won. And if the choice was between what was best for the parent company or the customer, the customer won.

The management approach, amazingly consistent despite the parade of owners and CEOs, was benevolently autocratic. Managers followed suit, while demanding loyalty to their department. Employees who demonstrated loyalty to the department were rewarded, and performance was almost always a secondary consideration. Suggestions were usually listened to, then discarded as undoable. Critical, open discussion was not permitted. Sarcasm and anger were accepted as the norm.

SCC's managers and employees did not make decisions well and almost never implemented what was decided. Management did not have a preferred, consistent decision-making process. They varied the process not on situational need, but on who was present and how politically critical the decision was. The TQM effort to establish a critical thinking process was never supported long enough to make a difference.

Informal Organization

SCC's managers and employees described the informal organization as close knit, powerful, vicious, nasty, and destructive. The informal organization was dysfunctional, keeping itself and the organization in disarray. The informal organization turned on each of its members, ensuring that no one would be able to advocate change without recrimination. The staff viewed this strategy as self-protective, fending off unwanted changes advocated by unwanted owners. In reality, the strategy was self-destructive.

No one was immune from the grapevine's relentless nasty stories about what they did and why they did it. A new Marketing and Sales director was hired in 1993, and before he arrived for his first day of work everyone knew his salary, the cost of moving him from a different region of the country, and why he had left his last position. Within days of beginning work, he was approached by several employees who said that they resented him and were angry that he was at SCC. They felt that SCC could not afford him, that he was a spoiled brat from a big company, and that he was greedy for negotiating a relatively high salary and a standard moving package.

SCC employees explained their nasty behavior toward him by rationalizing that he was new to the company and therefore would not be of immediate help. They thought that the company really needed more manufacturing help, not more sales help. Several employees even understood that they were being organizationally, self destructive, but few were willing to stop their behavior. The few that did try were ridiculed by their peers, and accused of trying to support the wrong side.

SCC's informal organization also stereotyped each employee, describing each employee in negative, unflattering terms. Each employee had publicly acknowledged strengths and weaknesses that everyone knew and discussed. The informal organization pressured employees not to improve or grow professionally, ridiculing their attempt to break out of their assigned stereotype. This informal organization behavioral pattern was a major influence in stopping the TQM program from having a positive, long-lasting impact. The TQM coordinator, a former manufacturing supervisor, was perceived as unable to know anything about quality or organizational change, despite attending an extensive TQM training program. After all, since he only knew one section of the manufacturing operation, how could he know ways to improve decision-making, improve quality in order-taking, or use new methods to measure effectiveness.

Paradoxically, the informal organization could also be very protective and caring about individuals. No matter how poorly an individual was treated in the work place by the informal organization, employees always took care of each other outside of it. If someone became sick, a group of employees would immediately go to work assessing what help was needed, and making sure it was given. SCC employees were very proud of how they cared for their own, helping regardless of the personal cost.

SCC's informal organization was a microcosm of the company as a whole. It was a collection of frightened people, who were fearful of change because they might lose what they had. Yet, they did not like what they had, and so they found themselves in a self-destructive pattern of defending what they did not like, and disliking their behavior. For SCC's employees, the only way not to break the self-destructive pattern and still feel like healthy human beings was to take care of each other outside of the workplace.

Culture

SCC's culture reinforced its negative image of itself. No one overtly tried to set a strategy for the culture component. The culture simply reflected SCC's own image of itself, a barely competent, marginal business that was living on past accomplishments. The image was pervasive throughout the company and its facilities.

The manufacturing floor was dirty and messy. The supervisors explained that it was as clean as it could be, that you had to understand that making coatings was a dirty process. The offices were poorly lit, with dark panel walls. The building was usually too hot or too cold for most employees. The walls, when not decorated with functional hangings like maps, and engineering drawings, were left bare.

Few employees belonged to any professional associations, and leadership in associations that employees participated in, was discouraged. Samples of past products lined the main conference room, but were not displayed with pride. Typically, they were tossed on a corner, along with several other products, creating a disorderly look. The overhead slide screens in the conference rooms were tattered and broken, the flip chart holders old and rickety, and the window dressings stark and dirty.

Analysis of SCC

SCC had none of the four characteristics typical of flexible organizations. First, the organization as whole reflected, at best, only a few of the dynamics of its market, and the needs of its customers. Second, the successive genetic cores were usually focused on their own needs and seldom able to gain a perspective on the whole organization. They were unable to see the organization as a continuously changing, living entity. Rather, the leadership viewed SCC in static terms.

Third, the genetic core was unaware that a change in one component or subcomponent would trigger change in all the others. Thus, managers or employees would make an improvement in one area, but soon find that the improvement withered and people returned to working in the less effective way. The organization was continually returning to its original homeostasis. None of the CEOs or managers understood that SCC could not change significantly by partial interventions. The whole company needed to be reinvented, creating a new strategic alignment and component congruency.

Fourth, SCC's past and current leadership never understood the need for continuous change. This lack of ability to see the need for change was somewhat contradictory for a company that made its living by creating chemical compounds through a strong R&D function. The chemical compounds and coatings were always changing by intention, however, the genetic core's legacy was that the organization was viewed as a static, stable entity.

In short, the genetic core was unaware that the SCC was a living entity that continuously changed, just as all living organisms do. Therefore, SCC became a rigid, dysfunctional organization and a living hell for most of its employees. Caught in a dysfunctional system that they were unable to change, the employees turned on themselves, fighting, blaming, and subverting each other. And while the employees were focused on the internal issues, the market and the customers left SCC with only its past accomplishments to be proud of and its future in doubt.

Chapter 5
A Flexible Organization in Action

"The secret of success is consistency to purpose."

— Benjamin Disraeli

Overview

Flexible organizations are in a continual state of flux, realigning to new developments in the market, and shifting intra-component and inter-component congruency. If inflexible organizations are caught in a rigid homeostasis; flexible organizations create and maintain a fluid balance. Management in inflexible organizations prefer calmness and stability; management in flexible organizations strive for purposeful motion and rebalancing.

The trademark of the flexible organization is the paradox of shifting realities, the recognition that all components need to be as congruent as possible and will never be congruent. Flexible organizations escape a rigid homeostasis because their management views the market as continually throwing stones into the pond, creating unending cycles of ripples that permanently alter the pond. In flexible organizations, management's function is to recognize the stones as they are thrown, and adjust strategy and congruency accordingly.

If captured in photographic snapshot, flexible organizations appear to be unaligned and incongruent, however, if they are photographed on videotape, they appear to be constantly shifting and adjusting to external and internal influences and changes. Flexible organizations create a new definition of stability, continually adjusting.

Destroying the Myth of the Unchangeable
Internal Auditor: A Flexible Organization in Action

Background

Many companies and most of the Fortune 100 expended a great deal of effort in the late 1980's and 90's reducing the size and scope of their corporate service departments. The efforts were typically started to reduce cost as companies searched for ways to remain competitive. Shrinking the staff, and the services of their corporate staff was an obvious strategy. It seldom altered their core competence, was politically easy to accomplish, and generated significant cost savings.

Despite a mandated need from the Federal government and company Board of Directors, internal audit departments are a target of the current cost cutting. Many Fortune 100 companies are demanding that their internal audit departments become more efficient, doing more with less. They must provide more value for less, and have been drastically downsized, while being asked to do more. The pressures are so great on internal audit departments, that for several years Internal Audit executives, like other corporate function executives, have formed benchmarking groups. They compare best practices, and develop approaches and strategies to recreate the mission of internal auditing. The benchmarking groups also serve as support groups for executives wrestling with the twin problems of doing more for less and reinventing themselves. To many, creating a flexible organization was the best way to manage these twin problems.

As an experienced financial executive, the new vice president of the Internal Audit Department (CIA) of a leading pharmaceutical company foresaw the need to build a flexible organization. Over a period of four years, he led his department on a journey to become a flexible, responsive organization. When appointed vice president of CIA, he was charged with changing the department's traditional role of financial police. The new mission for CIA was two-fold: (1) to remain as financial police, and (2) to become business advisors to the company. The Board was now demanding that the CIA build the contradictory role needed to maintain appropriate financial control, and add value to the corporation.

The vice president was charged with reducing costs steadily over a four year period. The current CIA budget was at an all time high. All Corporate finance departments were to be reduced in size and budget, and

CIA, as one of the biggest corporate financial departments was to be trend setter in demonstrating their commitment to meeting corporate objectives.

CIA had a corporate-wide reputation as being a great place to work (it was frequently referred to as the country club), if you were in favor with the former vice president. The former CIA vice president was an autocrat who wielded vast external and internal power. CIA's mission was to ensure and maintain a financial security throughout the world-wide corporation. The Audit executives knew all the irregularities, financial games, and outright misappropriations that had occurred in the company. They were in a position to make or break careers. Just the threat of having to face an unscheduled internal audit was enough to make most executives cringe. The power of the office enabled the former vice president to manage in whatever way he chose. He chose to manage autocratically and to reward his staff with perks like managerial conferences in resort locations. Thus CIA earned its the reputation as the country club.

When the new vice president arrived, he found that the CIA department had become a rigid organization. Its strategy was to routinely and consistently audit every one of the corporate entities, identifying any and all financial irregularities. The auditors visited the corporate entities in teams of five and six. Roles within the teams were clearly defined, with the experienced auditors performing the complex and challenging analyses, and the less senior auditors doing the menial data gathering chores. The auditors' product was a report produced two to three weeks after the on-site visit by the team. The report was sent to the ranking financial officer of the corporate entity.

Audit directors, who had the final responsibility for authorizing the content of the report, seldom encouraged discussion of the results with the company's financial officers. The report focused on compliance, with specific recommendations that had to be implemented prior to the next audit. The recommendations had the authority of the audit committee and a committee of the Board of Directors behind them. Failing to implement a recommendation could be a career-ending decision for a financial executive. Additionally, there was little escape. The company's officers first line of appeal was to the vice president of CIA.

Market Niche and Strategy: Old Department

The Department's overt mission was to ensure compliance by periodic inspection, and its covert mission was to be a constant threat to would be financial malfeasance. The Department's strategy to accomplish the mission was to:

- ❑ thoroughly understand the basic business of each corporate entity;
- ❑ intimately know the financial and information systems of each entity;
- ❑ thoroughly examine each entity's records on a periodic basis;
- ❑ create a reputation as a tough, reliable, impossible to elude audit department.

The focus of the department was on ensuring compliance. What was best for the auditee was never a factor in the Department's considerations. The vice president and the directors focused on how to produce the best possible audit of each subsidiary. Like most auditors, they believed that their product was the audit report.

Market Niche and Strategy: Creating a Flexible Organization

The Department's new mission, to be the financial police and business advisors, demanded that the new vice president begin by redefining what internal audit could be. He had to stretch the professional imaginations of an internal audit department that was already considered highly competent and effective. Concurrently, he had to begin to reduce costs to comply with corporate cost reductions.

In addition to all the usual problems of managing change, three major factors confounded the complexity of changing the internal audit department:

- ❑ Many internal auditors as individuals, are educated and acculturated to view issues as right or wrong,
- ❑ internal auditors are taught that alterations to normal procedure are suspicious and possible indicators of potential financial problems, and

❑   internal audit departments are responsible to the audit committee for ensuring ultimate fiscal compliance for the entire corporation.

In short, these factors create an atmosphere where most are suspicious of change. Change for the internal auditor means an increased likelihood of financial error, and perhaps even malfeasance. And because they are ultimately responsible for the auditee's behavior, change can jeopardize them from carrying out their professional mandate. Consequently, the new vice president faced the formidable task of converting a purposefully rigid department into a flexible organization.

The department staff's challenge was to learn to be more efficient at what they currently did, learn to be business advisors, and significantly reduce operating costs. The strategy to achieve these goals was to first improve the department's strength, auditing, and then learn business advising. Cost reductions would come as everyone learned to be more efficient, discovering how to improve the auditing process by doing less.

Genetic Core

The department's genetic core had historically just been the vice president. As a strong message that he intended to make significant changes in the department, the new vice president redefined and expanded the genetic core to include the directors. Knowing that mandating the changes required by Corporate Finance would only stiffen resistance to

Internal Audit Hierarchy
Vice-President
Directors
Managers
Supervising Auditors
Senior Auditors
Auditors
Assistant Auditors

the change, he decided to gain the full support of his direct reports. He understood that the real change needed was not that of achieving corporate compliance, but rather a deeper change that came from within the employees of the department. He also understood that the genetic core would lead the change, and would need to define it in familiar and understandable terms.

Almost immediately, he and the directors began to lay the framework for the new flexible organization in their staff meetings. Working together, they developed a mission, vision, and philosophy statement that set the tone for the new organization. After much discussion, they all concurred that they were embarking on an unending journey. The starting point was redefining the role and the process of internal auditing.

The new genetic core was, at first glance, marginally different from the old genetic core. Although clearly larger in size, it was composed of the directors from the previous regime, all of whom had been close advisors to the former vice president. Additionally, the new vice president had started his career with the company as an internal auditor in the department, and throughout had been friendly with the former vice president. The significant difference between the previous regime and this one was the new vice president's commitment to fulfill his paradoxical mission.

The genetic core's members were experienced financial professionals and highly respected auditors. The vice president had twenty years experience in financial management, and had just recently been Chief Financial Officer of one of the corporation's most rapidly growing companies. The four directors were all experienced internal auditors, each having begun their careers in public accounting and then moving to the corporation. Each had worked his or her way up through the internal audit career ladder, proving their abilities through the three levels of staff work, and as supervising seniors, and finally as managers.

The directors' careers in the corporation's internal audit department were at a dead-end. They had been caught in a double bind by the changes sweeping through the corporation: remain at their current level or leave the department or the company to have an opportunity to be promoted. The corporate Chief Financial Officer, performing his role in instituting major change, had decided that future vice presidents of internal audit must have operating financial management experience, preferably as CFOs of an operating company. He and his team felt that the vice president of internal audit position needed someone who understood the operating issues, the pressures to perform, and the impact of an audit on the operating company. His decision effectively capped the career opportunities within the department of each of the directors. The former career track of remaining in the department and striving to become the vice president was now gone. They must leave the department to advance their careers.

Consequently, the directors had to reassess their career objectives. If they decided to remain in internal audit, they had already reached their highest position. If they sought financial jobs elsewhere in the corporation, they must relocate their families, reorient their professional interests, and compete against proven financial managers to find a position. No matter what they decided, they had to make significant professional changes.

Caught in the larger changes sweeping the corporation, the genetic core's directors had to lead and guide the mandated change, or loose any chance of career advancement. If they ignored the mandate to change, the cost cutting pressures would force the CFO to replace them. If they resisted the change, they would lose the vice president's performance recommendation, essential to any move within the company. The only way to succeed was to change as individuals and to lead the change within the department. The double bind of having to change no matter what they did, forced them to discover new ways to accomplish the department's expanded mission.

Philosophy

Prior to the new vice president's arrival, the department did not have a published philosophy. The new vice president, in conjunction with the directors, developed a philosophy intended to inspire, set high standards, and move the department in a new direction. The management team developed the philosophy with great care. The team was aware that they were setting a new course for the department, and that a well-crafted, clear philosophy was vital to achieving their goals.

The management team planned to use the philosophy as the guiding set of values, setting the standard for all aspects of individual, team, and organizational life. The philosophy's beliefs were used as key criteria in designing the new, flexible organization. Over time the philosophy became ingrained into the daily strategic and tactical decision-making process within the department. On a strategic level, the philosophy guided all major decisions. The mission and vision set the conceptually desired outcome, and the beliefs set the parameters of how to reach the outcomes.

The department's vision, mission, and philosophy[14] were clearly articulated as follows:

Vision: We will strive to perform our responsibilities at the highest possible level. We will develop an organization that has five key attributes:

---

[14] The mission, vision, and philosophy has been paraphrased to maintain confidentiality.

❑   Providing leadership

We will lead by using technology to update our audit approach to provide the corporation with quality audits. We will lead by example, encouraging full participation by all members of our staff.

❑   Setting Professional Standards

We will develop and maintain the highest degree of trust and integrity with our customers and staff. We will strive to be respected and viewed as a source of highly talented individuals for the entire corporation.

❑   Encouraging Initiative

We will encourage innovation and initiative. We must develop and use a diversity of ideas. We will recognize those who are innovative and accept responsibility for their actions. All of us must consider mistakes as challenges to learn from.

❑   Building In Quality

We will excel in all aspects of our work by using the corporate quality process. We enhance our customer's performance by delivering quality services and information.

❑   Creating Teamwork

Building trust and teamwork based on mutual respect is essential.

Mission: Our purpose is to assist corporate and operating management in performing their responsibilities by giving them objectives insights, analyses, appraisals, observations, and recommendations relating to improving control.

Internal auditing observes and reports on business integrity, operational efficiency, and financial reporting accuracy. Additionally, internal auditing should:

- ❑ Avoid duplication of work with the independent public accountants.
- ❑ Investigate compliance of the regulations of the professional organizations, governmental agencies, and legislative actions.
- ❑ Identifying potential profit and cost improvement opportunities with operating management.
- ❑ Communicate control concerns and techniques to all operating units.
- ❑ Develop our staff as a pool of managerial talent for the corporation.

All department staff members were expected to conduct their professional life within the parameters set by the vision, mission, and philosophy statement. Staff and management discussed the implications of the philosophy in servicing customers, collaborating with each other, and interacting with other departments. The philosophy became a living standard, the organizational glue. It became the conceptual blueprint for redesigning the department into a flexible organization. When developing a new evaluation system, for example, the philosophy's beliefs were included in the criteria that the new system must meet. After it was created, the new evaluation system was reviewed and tested by its two sets of internal customers, the staff and the managers.

In addition to the publicly articulated philosophy, the new vice president added one simple belief. Prior to making significant decisions, particularly on sensitive issues with customers or key personnel issues, managers and staff were to ask themselves, "How would I like to be treated in this situation?" This philosophical belief became the guiding principal in designing the downsizing and restructuring plan. It also became the cornerstone for developing a department that fostered openness, honesty, and integrity. By using it to guide his decisions, the new vice president earned the respect and trust of his staff, a mandatory ingredient in all flexible organizations.

Formal Organization

The new vice president was confronted with a particularly difficult problem in addressing the formal organization. The department's seven organizational layers were clearly an anachronism (see chart on page 79). He had to flatten the organization to reach the cost-reduction objectives and the most obvious layer to remove was the director level. However, the directors held much of the power in the organization, having built a cadre of managers and staff that they had trained, mentored, and promoted over the years. To remove the director layer from the organization, he had to shift the power from the directors to the managers, shift the managers' focus away from pleasing the directors to meeting the needs of the customers, and find a way to retain the expertise and experience of the directors within the organization. Adding to this challenge, he had to begin the process with the directors.

Applying his principle of "How would I like to be treated," the new vice president simply involved the directors in solving the problem. He and the directors, based on their discussions and decisions in creating the vision, mission, and philosophy, designed a hierarchical structure that was intended to provide the maximum amount of flexibility to meet customer needs and the minimum amount of interference in serving customers. More concretely, the department was to change from a hierarchy based on expertise and experience reflected in organizational rank to expertise and experience reflected in how close the staff were to the customer.

Following this guideline, the new vice president determined that the directors were the staff members who had the most expertise. He challenged them to redesign their jobs to emphasize their auditing expertise and minimize their management responsibilities. In response, the directors restructured their jobs to have a great deal of interaction with customers, working with operating company executives to make improvements. This shift in their job descriptions helped meet the department's mandate to provide financial advice. The change in the director's responsibilities cascaded downward in the organization. The managers' and auditors' job responsibilities also changed. Managers assumed the primary responsibility for leading and managing the audit teams. They became more heavily involved on-site with audits, and staff assumed more day to day operational logistical and management duties.

This decision had significant implications for the department. It established the principle that any de-layering would not be done solely for cost reduction, but rather first to meet customer needs by developing and maintaining the highest expertise possible. Second, it redefined the role of management as keepers of expertise and knowledge. Third, it established that the underlying foundation was once again the department's vision, mission, and philosophy. The new vice president and the directors were interlocking the components of the organization by making them congruent, linking the department's philosophy firmly with the underlying principles of the formal organization.

The other sub-components of the formal organization were redesigned in the same manner, with extensive staff involvement. Directors and managers at the annual planning process reviewed the organization for congruency, identified which areas were incongruent, and established task forces of managers and staff to develop new designs. The task forces, redesigned the evaluation system, the extrinsic rewards, the training opportunities, the formal mentoring system, and the job descriptions and responsibilities.

The results from the work done by the new vice president, directors, and the task forces created a flexible, leaner formal organization. The results cascaded down throughout the organization. As the directors shifted their role from a traditional, hierarchical one, to keepers and nurturers of the expertise, the managers assumed greater responsibility for the audit process and results.

For example, in the old regime, a support staff member made all the travel arrangements for the staff. The support staff member reported to the director in charge of administration and was responsible for arranging travel and managing the costs. After the redesign, this position was eliminated. Each audit team appointed a staff member to make the travel arrangements, and the team was responsible for minimizing travel costs. The benefits were direct. A bureaucratic position was eliminated, decreasing organizational rigidity. The director was freed to focus more on customers, and staff were required to be responsible and accountable for their own spending. As a result, staff learned to make more of their own decisions, gained greater control of how they traveled, reducing a major contentious issue of the past.

In the new structure, standing committees of managers and staff members developed the audit schedule and assigned staff to audits. Staff members at all three levels asked for and were given greater responsibilities in the audit process, and greater latitude in decision making on-site, during the audit. A new extrinsic set of rewards was developed that encouraged individual and team effort. The new vice president awarded gift certificates to staff members who were deemed to have done work above and beyond requirements, such as working nights to replace a peer who had fallen ill during an out-of-town audit. The rewards, although seemingly insignificant and corny, symbolized the shift from the organization being responsible for an individual's behavior to the individual being responsible for his/her own behavior within the department's philosophical guidelines.

Information, Technology, and Work Processes:

The management team's strategy for the information, technology, and work process component was to:

❑ use the information systems to continually convey and reinforce the philosophy,
❑ use technology to create flexibility and innovation, and
❑ periodically redesign the work process to take advantage of new technological opportunities and new service opportunities from the evolving role of the audit department.

These broad strategies for the component had a profound impact on how staff and managers worked. In the information sub-component, the management team felt that department-wide communication was poor. Consequently, they decided to drastically redesign the communication system from a "let it filter down from the top" approach to a more structured approach, ensuring that information was disseminated. They instituted quarterly department meeting at which attendance was mandatory. The department's four sub-groups were also required to meet quarterly, discussing business and professional issues. To improve one-on-one communication, managers were required to meet quarterly with each of their staff members to discuss professional concerns, career issues, and departmental issues.

The new vice president established an open door policy that was soon emulated by the directors and managers. The results of management team meetings were summarized and distributed throughout the department. All task forces published their meeting minutes on E-mail and distributed hard copy. Prior to implementation, task force recommendations were shared in open, come if you like, forums, with discussion and input encouraged.

The increased communication significantly contributed to building a flexible organization. Traditionally divided into sub-groups that reflected the different segments of the corporations business, the audit staff had always been cliquish. The meetings began to break down the walls between the sub-groups, encourage more discussion on professional issues, and encourage learning. It also helped standardize the audit approach between sub-groups, and provided opportunities for staff to be promoted across sub-groups.

The technology area was also greatly changed. Shortly after arriving in the department, the new vice president began to purchase laptop computers for all audit staff members. The laptops enabled an audit team to produce the audit report on site, decreasing the report writing cycle time, and giving the auditee the report while the auditors were still on site and available for in-depth discussion. The staff were able to accomplish this objective in a relatively short time, increasing customer satisfaction, reducing costs, and improving customer acceptance of the results, increasing the likelihood that they would implement the recommendations.

Issuing audit reports on-site also had several other significant affects. The need for clerical help was greatly reduced, and the new vice president and directors soon saw that most clerical positions would no longer be needed (a significant cost reduction). Second, the quality of the audit reports improved as the final report was written when the data was still fresh in everyone's mind. Additionally, the team had the opportunity to review it together, ensuring a higher degree of accuracy, and everyone on the team felt responsible for the report. Third, the writing process became a learning process for younger staff members, who were now much more involved in the writing and presentation process. The entire audit process became more flexible, as it became less dependent on clerical staff who were not directly involved with the auditee, and more directly connected with the staff who did the research and analysis.

Behavior

If the philosophy of the department is the organizational glue, then the behavior is the brush that management uses to apply the glue. The strategy for the behavior component was to live the values and lead the change by role-modeling the new way of working. This was a difficult assignment for highly analytic, task focused professionals.

Over time, the new vice-president and the directors developed four strategies to change behavior and then embed it into the new way of working. First, they rewarded those managers and staff members who exhibited the new behavior on a consistent basis. Second, they promoted cognitive learning of new behaviors by making time available for skills development course work. Third, they openly discussed their behavior and the behavior of others, analyzing its helpfulness in achieving the department's goals. Fourth, they built the expected behavioral requirements into the evaluation process.

As expected, the new vice president led the behavioral change. From the time he took over the department, he role modeled behavior consistent with the articulated, philosophical values. In the beginning, he confused everyone. The directors, managers, and staff had not encountered anyone who was willing to be as different as the new vice president. They did not trust his statements at face value. When he said, "How would I like to be treated in this situation?" in response to managers inquires about how to reprimand a staff member, the managers thought that he was playing a clever developmental game, avoiding the question, being hopelessly naive, or perhaps all three.

Few believed that he meant his statements literally and that his open, honest responses could be believed. The directors were shocked that he discussed his plans to downsize the department by attrition and openly stated that their roles had to change. They believed he must be misunderstanding the situation, because no one would share that kind of information with those staff members whose jobs were affected. However, as he persevered, the behavior became infectious. The informal leaders began to follow his lead and press others to behave in the new way.

The vice president and directors redesigned the training courses offered for the staff. In addition to the corporation's courses, they added specific courses on managing, teamwork, and communication. The courses were used to create a common language and a base level of understanding. Staff was encouraged to attend the classes, and managers were required to attend.

In department, sub-group, and team meetings, formal and informal leaders discussed behaviors. Managers and team leaders discussed different ways to manage situations, comparing different approaches with different personalities. Teams discussed behavior that helped the team and hindered the team, identified ways to change unhelpful behavior, and created informal support to assist staff and managers in the change.

Finally, the task force that re-vamped the evaluation process added behavioral expectations that were measurable and quantifiable. The task force, composed of managers and staff members of all levels, set standards that specified individual and group behaviors. Additionally, the task force linked with another to begin to design the 360° evaluation system necessary to reinforce the desired behaviors.

Informal Organization

The informal organization's purpose was twofold: (1) provide peer support, and (2) provide a social life. The informal organization, recognizing the essential balance and health of the department, was focused on meeting staff needs that the rest of the organization could not. The informal organization provided the peer support that enabled employees and managers to gain additional information and understanding of their career and job options. The interpersonal connections between staff members were strong because of their extensive traveling and the subsequent extended time together away from home. Staff members knew each other well, bonding together to accomplish their tasks and to survive in locations in which they were always the stranger and unwelcome visitor.

The informal organization's support was extensive. Experienced auditors taught the new auditors how to survive the travel, how to manage hostile receptions by frightened auditees, and how to manage their managers. Informal mentors guide new auditors through the ropes of proving themselves as auditors, showing them the pitfalls of auditing, and boosting their self-confidence when they had to report to executives.

The informal organization, as typical of most healthy organizations, had a complete, unofficial, and oral evaluation of all the managers and directors. Each manager's style was well known, backed by a set of examples that illustrated the style in practice. Informally, staff learned who they would prefer to work for, and made deals to become a member of their desired manager's staff. And of course, the staff had a well-known and sophisticated system to trade world-wide audit assignments. Exotic, warm locations were always at a premium and highly sought after. Staff members strove to earn the experience and credentials so they could trade assignments.

The informal organization also became the social network for many of the staff. With so little time spent at home, the auditors seldom had time for a social life. Co-workers became not only colleagues but also peers to socialize with, to explore new places with, and to date. The grapevine was full of personal chatter and even the most socially-active staff members were amazed at how a team of auditors in Hong Kong would know who was dating whom in Belgium before anyone knew back at the home office.

Culture

The department's culture was professional and formal. The new vice president chose to maintain the long-standing formal culture because it reinforced the department's need for high professional standards, and was congruent with the overall culture of corporate headquarters. The dress code remained conservative, tailored, and well manicured, with business suits as the standard. All public interaction was unfailingly polite.

However, the new vice president and directors worked on reducing the differences and privileges based solely on rank. Managers maintained open door policies, closing doors only to discuss personnel issues or highly sensitive client information and issues. Management retreats were changed from week long sessions in resort locations to three and four day working sessions at nearby conference centers. Staff and managers shared the services of the remaining support staff, normally on a first-come, first-served basis.

Staff members were assigned to work on all departmental task forces, were given responsible assignments in redesigning the department, and made presentations to the whole staff on their work. Experience and expertise were valued, often as much as rank and length of service. Perhaps most telling, the department was a rainbow of human colors. The new vice president, directors, and managers carefully and methodically recruited staff from as many ethnic and language groups as possible. The executive team felt that the best way to serve a global corporation with locally-controlled companies, was to recruit and train auditors from as many different nationalities as possible.

The culture reflected this mix. For example, executives had historically placed great emphasis on writing excellent English because the audit report was the department's product. Every manager was well versed in English grammar, vocabulary, and phrasing. Each prided him/herself on the ability to write a well-crafted, concise, and precise audit report.

However, the new vice president, directors, and managers, through the input of the staff, began to realize the language centrixness of using English as the primary language. They began to wonder if a CFO, who spoke only limited English, but was fluent in Mandarin Chinese really cared how well-crafted the English was in the audit report. This realization triggered a major discussion and ultimately support from the new vice president, directors, and managers to reexamine perfect English's importance to good auditing and its importance in evaluating English as a second language speaking staff members. The re-evaluation process was an outstanding example of how the department had become a flexible organization working to change itself.

Case Analysis

The Internal Audit Department was neither a perfect organization nor one without conflict. Like all flexible organizations, some People-Centered Organization® components were more congruent with the department strategy than others. Clearly, the department's behavior component needed improvement at all levels of the organization. Not only did the managers need to learn how to manage the non-technical side of the business better, but the entire staff needed to know how to better work in flattened hierarchical teams.

In the formal organization, the new vice president and directors needed to resolve the issue of the supervising senior auditors. Supervising senior auditors were experienced team leaders who were expected to assume some, but not all, the roles of managers. Although the new vice president and directors felt that supervising senior auditors were not on a separate level, the staff perception was different, as was the perception of the two supervising senior auditors. At the time of this writing, the issue was being ignored, a rare occurrence in the department.

The department had the four characteristics typical of flexible organizations. First, the organization as whole reflected the dynamics of its market and the needs of its customers. Second, the genetic core was aware that the department would always be changing and that change was the norm that must be accepted by all staff members. Third, the genetic core was aware that a change in one component or subcomponent would trigger change in all the others, thus the staff would be adjusting and improving the organization continuously. Fourth, the department had to involve as many interested staff members as possible in the continuous redesign process to ensure maximum flexibility. In short, the genetic core was aware that the department was a living entity that continuously changed like all living organisms.

The department, like any flexible organization, always was partially congruent and partially incongruent, as the components shifted to a new equilibrium. Like all living organisms, flexible organizations will always be incongruent when viewed in a static snapshot. They will be so because they are shifting to meet new challenges and mirror the changes in the market place. The trademark of the flexible organization is the inherent contradictiion in shifting realities, the recognition that all components need to be as congruent as possible and but will never be perfectly congruent.

For example, the technology sub-component in the department needed to shift again to keep pace with emerging remote auditing techniques. New computer technology had begun to enable auditors to review operating company records from afar, sitting at their own desks. The implications of this shift most likely will be as great as the shift from desk top only computing to laptop computing. If remote auditing produces the same high level of financial control as on-site auditing does, then the work processes will shift as much as they did when the staff began to issue on-site audit reports. This change will trigger the same degree of organizational change as before and the department will once again begin to redesign itself. Or perhaps the English as a Second Language issue will trigger the next major cycle. Only one thing is for certain, one of the major issues that currently faces the department will cause the next round of redesign.

Section Three
Changing Individuals and Teams in Flexible Organizations

"All is flux, nothing stays still."

Heraclitus
From *Diogenes Laertius, Lives of Eminent Philosophers.*

Introduction

The first section of this book, Chapters One through Three, discussed how organizations work and introduced People-Centered Organizations® as a way to view the organization of the future. Chapters One through Three had three central themes:

1. today's organizations and those of the future need to be flexible, altering strategies as needed, and shifting congruency to match the new strategies;
2. organizations are built around people; and
3. flexible organizations are in a continual state of flux as they alter strategies and balance congruency.

In Section Two, chapters Four and Five built on these themes by illustrating how two different organizations responded to their environment. SCC was not able to evolve past its initial genius, as it ignored the demands of its market and the capabilities of its competitors. On the other hand, the Internal Audit department was able to use the demands of its external environment to learn to become flexible. SCC demonstrated how an organization can become rigid, and the Internal Audit department showed how an organization can create a responsive organization.

Section Three adds depth to these themes by presenting a theoretical framework showing how the change processes in organizations, teams, and individuals are the same. Or more strongly stated, this Section argues that organizations and teams change the same way as people do. People alter strategies to meet new environmental demands, then shift their internal congruency in the same way as flexible organizations do. Teams also change in this way.

The change process for all three entities are interconnected (see basic principles of how organizations work in Chapter One). Individuals are a subset of teams and organizations, and teams are a subset of organizations. They can be conceived as three vertically stacked tiers, starting with the individual and moving upward to teams and organizations (See drawing #2). In flexible organizations, the focus for all three tiers is the organization's purpose and strategy. For the teams and individuals in the organization, the organizational tier is their external environment or market. The team tier is an external environment or market for the individual. Actions performed by anyone in any of the tiers has a ripple affect on everyone in any tier. Like the stone thrown into the pond analogy from Chapter Four, the ripples not only spread outward through the organization, they cascade downward to the teams and individuals, and then return upward to the teams and the organization.

Viewing the change process as the same and as interconnected for organizations, teams, and people has immense implications for leading, guiding, and managing companies. If executives understand how the change process works, and how they are interconnected, then executives can use this knowledge to increase their capability to build and lead flexible organizations.

Chapter Six will discuss how the change process in all three tiers is similar and how a change in any tier or any component affects all the others. Chapter Seven presents three case studies to illustrate how the three-tiered change process works at a company, team, and individual level.

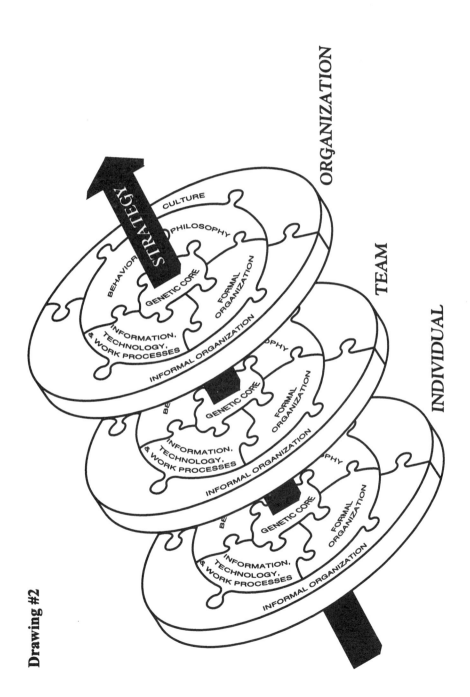

Drawing #2

Chapter 6
The Interplay Among Individuals, Teams, and Organizations

> *"Living system,* then, is a *metaphor* for a whole . . . for a sense of the summative quality, the greater than the parts. . . . It is a metaphor for the betweenness, for the sets of relationships, which we must sense, imagine, connect, create. Thus, living systems are like a moving holo gram again, constantly shifting planes and fields, there but not there."

Bunny S. Duhl
*From The Inside Out
and Other Metaphors*

The Process and Content of Change

Flexibility is the process of continually adapting to new realities, of developing new strategies congruent with a new or changed environment, and then realigning all aspects of the individual, group, or organization with the new strategy. The continuously adaptation process is the same for individuals, groups, and organizations. As living organisms, they follow the same steps in the change process. Although greatly different in size, they use similar and parallel constructs (the content of change) to decide what they should change.

Successful adaptation requires managing the transition from one strategy to the next as efficiently as possible. The steps in the transition process are:

1. Collect data from the external environment;
2. Organize the data;
3. Compare the newly collected data to previous data;
4. Determine how different and similar the two sets of data are; and
5. Decide if a change in strategy is needed.

In organizations, individuals collect data by looking laterally and vertically up through the tiers, assessing the actions and intentions of their peers, their team, and their organization. They analyze this newly collected data for consistency with previously collected data, determine differences and similarities, then decide to maintain or change their strategy. This three-tiered analysis is a continual process, usually conducted without conscious awareness, in all individuals, teams, and organizations.

They use eight constructs (ideas inferred from a set of concepts) to organize the data, make comparisons, and decide if, and what, they should change. Collectively, these eight constructs define who a person is, his or her personality. With some modification, the eight constructs also define the nature of a team and organization. The constructs are:

1. the nature of the world we live in,
2. what we are,
3. what we believe,
4. how we structure our lives,
5. how we behave,
6. how we process information and apply it to a situation,
7. who we know, and
8. what we value.

As individuals, teams, and organizations mature or age and as circumstances change, they adapt and continue to grow by modifying or adapting to changes in all eight constructs, ensuring that the changes are all congruent, and thereby supporting and reinforcing the new strategy.

Individual Change Process and Content

A young woman leaving high school and entering college needs to develop a new strategy for the tougher, more challenging environment. She needs to change key aspects in all eight constructs. She needs to recognize the new world she lives in (construct #1), needs to learn new behaviors (construct #5), such as study habits, to survive in a more challenging academic environment. She needs to discover new ways to analyze and structure data (construct #6). She needs to acquire new friends for her social network and allow some former relationships to fade (construct #7). She needs to reorganize her daily schedule (construct #4) to meet the new requirements of college. She will find that her beliefs about what is good and bad will change as she is exposed to different people and cultures, and new information (construct #3) and what she values from friends, education, and family changes also (construct #8). Undoubtedly, she will have to change her understanding and concept of who (construct #2) she is as she grows and adapts.

None of these changes will happen as smoothly as described. Few of her changes will happen simultaneously. Instead they will occur in response to external environmental stimuli and her ability and willingness to alter her strategies and balance herself internally. Like a flexible organization, her adaptation process will be in continual flux.

Through her years at college, she will find that the world she lives in constantly changes. The expectations of her professors become greater and the assignments more difficult. Concurrently, her view of her place in the world changes. She entered college overwhelmed and intimidated by the size, the academic challenges, the social freedom, and the independence and corresponding lack of family support. As she successfully completes each year, her feelings and perceptions of her world change. She becomes comfortable in meeting the academic and social challenges placed before her, she gains confidence that she can master the demands of college, and she begins to look beyond her college world to larger domains.

She has significantly changed who she was by changing the eight constructs. Her world view changes as she begins to view college as a step in a lifetime journey, peering ahead to the working world, further education, marriage, or all three. Her study habits are much different from what they were when she entered college. She has become more efficient in studying, having recognized how she learns and what she should learn. She can quickly identify trends and patterns in raw data, and recognizes many trends based on only a few pieces of significant data.

She has developed many new friendships and connected strongly with types of people she had never met before. She has been exposed to an unbelievable number of lifestyles, philosophies, cultures, and family values and dynamics. She has most likely experimented with several of the lifestyles and philosophies, been attracted to different cultures that seemed to better fit her personality and beliefs, and has found the pleasures and difficulties of living with people of different backgrounds.

She has adjusted to all the freedom that college offers, understanding that much of the free time is an illusion and that class work can easily fill sixty hours a week. She has gone through the various stages from wondering how to fill all the free time, to wondering how to complete her class work in so little time, to knowing how to balance the rigors of academia and the needs of an active social life. Her type of residence and its decorations have paralleled her growth. In her freshman year she lived in a dormitory, with randomly assigned rooms and roommates. The dorm room, with its standard furniture and limited space, was a metaphor for her freshman year. By her junior year, she was living with three of her best friends in an apartment filled with furniture they bought and decorated to reflect their views of the world.

Paradoxically, she is not the same person who entered college three years before and yet she is the same person. She has grown with her experiences in a new environment, adapting to her new world and changing her sense of who she is and what she believes in. She has discarded the behavior and beliefs of a high school student and adopted the behaviors and beliefs of a soon-to-be college graduate. She has built on who she was, consciously and unconsciously discarding the beliefs, behaviors, thinking processes, and friends that no longer fit her strategy to survive (and hopefully thrive) in her new environment.

If she maintains her physical and emotional health, she will continually repeat this pattern of flexibly changing and of renewing, for the rest of her life. She will discover that this cycle of continuous renewal will not only apply to her, but to the teams she works with and the companies she works in. She will find that she must make difficult choices between adapting completely to her work team or her company, or a compromise between the two.

Three-Tiered Change Analysis

In ten years, when she has worked in two or three different positions, she will be recruited for her education and experience by another company. Accepting the offer, she will join an already established professional work team. She will find that the team members have a collective view of their work world. Each member has a strong belief about the company's market, strategy, and capabilities. Each member has an equally strong view about the team's purpose, its strategy and its capabilities. The team has its own way of approaching problems, dealing with conflict, and communicating. Cultural pressures will most likely be strong, and established informal leaders will either support or compete with the formal team leaders. If she is like most employees, most of her job satisfaction or dissatisfaction will come because she likes or dislikes her immediate supervisor.[15]

However, if she is in a well-balanced, well-functioning company, she will find that she needs to assess how well her team's mission aligns with the company's mission and strategy. She will find herself analyzing how her team's performance furthers the company's objectives, how well it meets the customers needs. She will compare her team's philosophy to the company's philosophy, determining if there are any inconsistencies. She will examine the company's hierarchy, assessing whether the organizational structure helps or hinders her team in accomplishing its mission. She will watch to see how the pay structure motivates or de-motivates her colleagues, and of course, herself.

She will probably suggest an improvement in the way she goes about her assignments, and her supervisor's answer will tell her if the company is willing to change the work processes. She will request some information that few others have ever asked for, and again the supervisor's answer will tell her how much the company supports her using her mind or how much the company wants her to be a robot. She will use the company's informal network to learn all aspects of the company, from the CEO's preferences to the oral history of the company. She will learn who to contact when she needs something done in Finance, and whom to trust in Human Resources. At first, she will clearly see the cultural norms and biases of the company, and eventually, she will find that she sees them less well because she has absorbed them.

In short, she will be continually performing a three-tiered analysis that compares the company's organizational dynamics to her teams' dynamics and to her personal, inner dynamics. When she first joins the company, her analysis will be deliberate and she will be consciously aware of the her multi-variate comparisons. She will use her awareness to guide her learning process as she absorbs the demands of her role, the expectations of her team, and the functioning of her company. As she masters her job, understands her team, and becomes accustomed to her company, her conscious awareness of her three-tiered analysis will disappear. Instead, the analysis will become unconscious, as she becomes absorbed in the problems and challenges of the moment.

However, the analysis will always continue, assessing the dynamics and the interplay between the three tiers. Her unconscious mind will remind her conscious mind when the normal interplay patterns are broken when some new dynamic does not fit the pattern of the previous ones. She will then have to do her analysis deliberately, assessing what the change means to her career, role, wage, and daily work life. After determining the impact on her, she will make a similar assessment for her friends, colleagues, team, and the company. The outcome of her analysis will determine her response to the organizational changes.

Organization and Team Change Content

The eight key constructs that the young woman used in her three-tiered analysis are parallel concepts of the components in the People-Centered Organizations° framework. The following table illustrates their parallel nature.

Table 5   Comparison of Key Individual and Organizational Constructs

Individual Construct	Organizational Component
The nature of the world we live in	The market place
What we are	Genetic core
What we believe	Philosophy
How we structure our lives	Formal organization
How we behave	Behavior
How we process information and apply it to a situation	Information, technology, and work processes
Who we know	Informal organization
What we value	Culture

As the young woman's thinking demonstrated, the individual constructs are interlocked with the organizational components. The young woman analyzes and behaves in congruence with the larger system around her. How the organization is designed influences her behavior.

The influence is multi-directional, the young woman's behavior will impact the organization and its interactions with her. Suppose the young woman and her colleagues fail to produce a quality product and the product fails to make a profit for their company because of the quality problems. The organization's leaders then must make a choice between replacing the workers, or making a change in another component (see the interdependency section's example of developing new products in a manufacturer in Chapter Two, page 15). Either way, the leaders are changing the organization to respond to the young woman and her colleagues.

The individual constructs and the organizational components are also parallel to team constructs.

Table 6   Comparison of Key Individual, Team, and
Organizational Constructs

Individual Construct	Team Construct	Organizational Component
The nature of the world we live in	The larger organization	The market place
What we are	The team members	Genetic core
What we believe	The team's mission, and operating philosophy	Philosophy
How we structure our lives	How the team is organized, and its members's roles	Formal organization
How we behave	Team members's behaviors	Behavior
How we process information and apply it to a situation	How the team shares and process information, the technology it uses, and its work processes	Information, technology, and work processes
Who we know	The informal sub-groups	Informal organization
What we value	The team's working environment	Culture

The team is influenced from three directions, by the individuals within it, by the organization it is in, and by the interaction of its components. The influences come from below—the needs of its members—and from above—the demands of the organization. The horizontal influences come from the interdependency of its components, continually adjusting to be congruent.

The multi-directional influence among all three tiers is the key to building flexible, People-Centered Organizations®. Most normal, healthy humans make the three-tiered analysis on a regular basis and adjust most of their behavior accordingly.[16] It is simply a homeostatic process in action. Flexible organizations' genetic cores make the same kind of analysis, adjusting their organization to fit the demands of the marketplace, the demands of the teams within, and the needs of their people. A flexible organization's leaders understand the bi-directionality of the three-tiered analysis, using strategic alignment as the beginning point to building congruent organizations. They understand that organizations must be built on this well-documented phenomenon of people making intelligent decisions to meet their needs, and following their survival strategies.[17]

Consequently, executives can anticipate changes up and down the three tiers. They can anticipate how employees will respond to pay system changes, adjust the work processes at the organization level and the team level to accommodate the anticipated change in employee behavior. Executives building flexible organizations hire employees whose values

[16] See:

Milton Erickson, *Creative Choices in Hypnosis,* edited by Ernest L. Rossi and Margaret O. Ryan. New York: Irvington Publishers, Inc., 1992.

Jay Haley, *Leaving Home: The Therapy of Disturbed Young People,* New York: McGraw-Hill Book Company, 1980.

Salvador Minuchin, *Families and Family Therapy,* Cambridge, MA: Harvard University Press, 1974.

Bill O'Hanlon, "The Third Wave: The Promise of Narrative," *The Family Therapy Networker,* November/December 1994, pp. 18-29.

Ernest Rossi, *The Psychobiology of Mind-Body Healing,* New York: W. W. Norton & Company, Inc. 1986.

[17] See:

Frederick Hertzberg, ibid.

Douglas McGregor, *The Human Side of Enterprise,* New York: Mc-Graw Hill Book Company, 1967.

closely match those of the organization and who have the ability to create teams that are strategically aligned with the organization.

It is not executives alone who can build flexible organizations. Team members who can clearly see the need to shift colleague behavior to increase congruency can redesign teams and influence organizational components to drive the desired behavior. Teams, knowing that organizational functional barriers will block their efforts to accomplish a task, can begin a process to penetrate functional silos. If they are successful in knocking down the barriers, they will have created change in the organizational tier above them by changing the organization's structure. And they will have created change in the tier below them by changing individual behavior.

Chapter 7
Shifting to Flexibility

"Like all of Holmes' reasoning the thing seemed simplicity itself when it was once explained."

Sir Arthur Conan Doyle
The Stock Broker's Clerk

The homeostatic tendency for organizations, teams, and individuals to adapt to congruency up and down the three tiers is critically important for executives leading, guiding, and managing change. They can take advantage of homeostasis to:

1. shorten the time required for modifications at the organizational tier to cascade down to the team and individual tiers (or reduce the time required for the modifications to flow upward or outward);
2. make changes at the team or individual level when organizational change is temporarily blocked (or changes in any two tiers when the third is blocked); or
3. create organizational and team change by intervening at the individual level and allowing the changes to flow upward and outward (or intervening at the organizational or team tier to change individuals).

Building on their knowledge of the basic principles of how organizations work, and taking advantage of the three-tiered homeostatic process, executives have the capability to manage organizational change more precisely than ever before. The following three examples illustrate how executives have done this.

The first example, "Introducing A New Philosophy," demonstrates how an executive team was able to reduce the time lag between organizational change and team and individual change. It illustrates how a nimble genetic core took advantage of the need to redirect a division's mission to create more extensive change in all three tiers.

"Redesigning A Team's Work Processes," the second example, depicts a change process that focused on teams and spread to the individual and organizational tiers. Despite resistance to the team changes in the genetic core, the work processes modifications rippled throughout all three tiers.

The third example, "Building Around The Skills and Abilities of a New Team Member," discusses how a change in an individual's role had a positive and significant impact on her peers, her team, and eventually her organization.

Introducing a New Philosophy

Overview

Introducing a new organizational philosophy immediately creates a need to change the organizational components (change in the organizational tier), demands that teams reexamine how they work and what they are trying to accomplish (change in the team tier), and forces individuals to reexamine their roles and careers in the organization (change in the individual tier).

A telecommunication company's division executive team seized a change in mission as an opportunity to develop more efficient ways to work. They were able to develop a quick, efficient process to disseminate the new ways to work throughout the division, shortening the time for the change to cascade down and out the tiers. Speeding up the change process enabled the division's staff to quickly refocus on the new job at hand.

The division's executive team was appointed the same day that the division's mission was mandated to move from a national sales account management to an international account management responsibility. The new CEO and his executive team met for the first time on the eve of a previously scheduled three-day meeting of key managers. In a fast-paced, pressure-filled meeting, the executive team considered options on how to approach implementing the new mission.

Market Niche and Strategy

The executive team quickly reviewed the strategic situation. The division's market was fiercely competitive. The division's new strategy required that it expand its national scope to an international one, learn to work with a new overseas strategic partner, and reduce costs to remain price competitive. Corporate executives were demanding immediate results, a key reason they replaced the old executive team with the new one. To meet these demands, the executive team decided that they must shift the division's bureaucratic way of working to a more team based, performance focused one.

Tactically, the executive team understood that they had a very limited time to change the division enough to enable it to meet the new strategy. The company's culture was highly political with frequent changes in management that encouraged employees who did not like the current regime to wait until a new one was appointed. The staff were experts at avoiding changes introduced by new regimes. To have a chance to succeed, any significant change in working patterns would have to be linked to the new mission, which the staff viewed as mandatory. It was not an edict from a new management, but rather a change demanded by entry into new markets.

The executives believed that the shift to a new way of working might be successful while uncertainty about the political lifetime of their new team was high. They felt that the staff was willing to grant them a honeymoon period because of the change in mandate. This window of opportunity would delay dissatisfied key senior managers from beginning the business as usual process of lobbying with their sponsors at the corporate level to block the changes. The executive team was also aware that they some influential senior managers were already lobbying to stop announced promotions and reassignments. They needed to bypass these senior managers, who were politically-protected and highly committed to the status quo.

The executive team had two upcoming events that would allow them to circumvent the politics. The first was the three-day managers' meeting that started the next day. The second was the national sales conference scheduled six weeks later. The CEO decided to introduce the team-based, performance-focused concept to the managers in the upcoming meeting, and wait to see the reaction before planning the national sales conference.

The executive team linked the division's new mission to a new operating philosophy that articulated the basic principles of working in a team based, performance-focused work world. They explicitly stated that the division must reduce its bureaucracy and political fiefdoms. They also stressed that the division must provide outstanding customer service at a lower cost or be disbanded. In addition to developing the new philosophy, they redefined the role of departments and teams within the division to match the new philosophy.

Introducing the Change in Philosophy

The next day, the executives introduced the new mission and the new philosophy to the group of eighty managers. The managers, breaking into small groups, discussed the old mission and philosophy, compared it to the new, and identified blockages needed to be eliminated or overcome at the organizational, team, and individual levels. Working long hours for the next two days, the managers' groups developed proposed solutions to the blockages, coordinated their proposals with each other, and presented their proposals to the executive team. During the presentation process, the executive team and the managers jointly categorized the solutions into short, medium, and long-term ones.

The executive team, working late into the night, reviewed all the proposed solutions. They approved and authorized immediate implementation of those that required no capital expense. The other proposed solutions were reassigned to the managers' groups to develop detailed action plans specifying time frames, costs, and benefits.

The impact of introducing the new mission and the new philosophy to the managers was powerful and immediate. The new philosophy created a set of behavioral expectations for the executives and the managers. Because the managers' groups were charged with identifying blockages that prevented the division from achieving its mission, and developing ways to remove them, the participating managers correctly believed that the new executive team wanted significant change. Consequently, they expected the executive team to become an advocate for change and to provide ongoing support for the change.

The new philosophy also triggered a change in organizational behavior as the groups at the three-day meeting took action to improve the organization. Because the philosophy and executive behavior were congruent, the managers believed that change could really take place.

The natural leaders among the managers, seeing the opportunity to drive change, rose to the occasion and pushed their peers into action. And like the executive team, the natural leaders found that the new philosophy demanded that they behave in a different way, consistent with the philosophy.

As the natural leaders changed their behavior, reviving their leadership and participative management skills, they changed the behavior of the members of managers' groups. During the group meetings, many of the preassigned leaders focused on accomplishing the assigned tasks, pushing their opinions as the preferred solution, and stifling discussion and opposing points of view. The participants accepted this as the normal way to work, and began to become cynical. However, the natural leaders, reinforced by the coaching of executive team members, began to challenge the group process. Within hours, the group leaders began to change their autocratic styles to more participative ones. Encouraged, the group members began to challenge each other and their leaders. Team and individual behavior had already begun to shift.

As the executive team saw the managers change their behavior, identifying operating issues that had historically been problems and lowering long standing functional feuds to develop realistic and practical solutions, they were amazed and delighted. They began to understand that they had only one course of action: continue to harness the power of those that wanted to improve the organization. They also had to change their behavior. As the genetic core they had to behave consistently with the new philosophy, delegating authority and responsibility to subordinates rather than maintaining the control themselves. Additionally, they needed to make these changes immediately, so that the eighty assembled managers could see the behavior change.

The executive team was also aware that actually implementing the proposed solutions to the blockages was the only key to ensuring that the behavior change was more than an "off-site" phenomenon. The groups had identified issues such as commissions, contract management, common data bases, better sales tools and material, redesigned administrative processes, and clearer reporting relationships. The groups were recommending solutions to these issues that supported and were congruent to the new philosophy. Throughout the three-day meeting, the managers focused all discussions on the real purpose of the change, aligning the organization with the new mission and philosophy.

The New Philosophy Ripples Outward and Downward

Word quickly spread on the grapevine that something different was happening at this meeting. At first, staff back in the home offices did not differentiate between the "something different" and the hot news about the executive changes. Most staff members discussed the normal issues of who won, who lost, and what the impact would be on them. However, it soon became clear that indeed something different was happening at the three-day meeting. Participating managers began requesting information from their offices to determine recommendations to the identified problems at the meeting. They made telephone calls to staff requesting research on key sub-issues, stressing the importance of developing the analyses as soon as possible.

Back at the offices, many staff members were now very curious. The normal pattern of an executive management shift had been broken and they began to wonder why. Performing the three-tiered analysis, a few of the leaders back in the home offices began to analyze the bits and pieces of data that they were receiving. They realized that major, significant change was being planned and implemented at the three-day meeting. In an unprecedented action, some key leaders who had not been invited to the "off-site," or who had turned down the invitation because they were too busy, or who chose to attend more politically advantageous activities, changed their plans, flew to the "off-site" location, and joined the groups.

The impact of the late arrivers was enormous. Almost every one of the one thousand staff members who remained back in the home offices now knew that something extremely different and important was happening. And whatever was happening was as big as the change in the executive team. They also knew that it was exciting, as their peers who were attending the "off-site" shared some of the details with them. As they conducted their own three-tiered analysis, they began to realize that major change was being required by the new executive team. This executive team was truly requiring something different. This change was the opposite of most management successions where the new executive team rewarded past loyalties and consolidated their own power and control.

The new executive team demanded that the staff began to use their own judgment, forgo the loyalty to bureaucratic fiefdoms, and focus on providing better service to the internal and external customers. Rather amazingly, the staff began to react to this message quickly. Their three-tiered analysis told them that the change was significant and had a real chance to succeed. Never before had they seen such a break in the executive pattern, nor seen managers so excited and involved in projects, nor, perhaps most powerfully, seen politically connected and protected managers and directors join an "off-site" already in progress.

Staff members behaved in various ways to the change that was sweeping the division. Some of the staff immediately decided that they did not like the change, were not willing to live through this regime's requirements, and began searching for a way to be transferred to another division. Others rushed to support their colleagues at the three-day meeting, obtaining the requested information, and consulting with their peers electronically. Most however remained skeptical, adopting a "wait and see" approach which had historically served them all well. Nonetheless, even they were amazed at the changes that were reputed to be taking place at the "off-site." Although skeptical about the permanence of the changes, they were aware that these changes might really happen, and they needed to be prepared to change. If nothing else, they had never seen so many of their peers rushing to move out of the division. Or for that matter, other division staff asking to be transferred in.

The executive team, through their contacts in the home offices and in the groups, were aware of the different types of activity and the excitement. The momentum for change, started by their decision on the first night of the three-day meeting to implement a new way of working, spread from them to the whole organization. The momentum cascaded down and through the organization, gaining more energy, and engulfed the reluctant executives on its way back up the organization. The executive team realized that they had to grab the momentum, harness it to more concrete, tangible changes, and then send it back down through the organization again. To do this, they immediately implemented several of the group recommendations. They explained their logic to the "off-site" participants, ensuring that the participants understood the business constraints and the business logic supporting each decision.

By the end of the meeting, the executives were overwhelmed by the positive reaction to the new philosophy. They were also amazed at how much work and change had already been accomplished by the managers' groups. They unanimously agreed to undertake two major steps to maintain and build on the momentum of the change. They believed it was imperative to keep the managers' groups working and to design the national sales conference as a follow-up to the three-day managers' meeting.

Building Momentum Between the Meetings

Consequently, the executive team requested the groups to further develop the medium and long-term recommended solutions. The managers' groups identified other staff members with special expertise to join them to create fully-developed solutions that detailed costs, benefits, implementation processes, and time frames. Their group assignments were given priority over daily business activities, and group members who could not commit the time needed were asked to find replacements for themselves. At the annual sales conference, the groups were to present their recommendations to the executive team and then to the 500 sales conference participants. No one left the "off-site" thinking that the change to a new way of working was a short-term management program. Every one understood that the executive team had just committed to totally redesigning the sales conference, which was only six weeks away, at considerable cost and effort.

The groups continued to work back in their home offices. They recruited key staff members who had specialized knowledge, increasing the quality of their proposed solutions. After four weeks, the groups convened at a brief "off-site" to report progress to the executive team. Again the executive team demanded more quality, better analysis, and detailed impact studies. But the executive team clearly supported the groups and their solutions. They also repeated their decision to allow the groups to develop the solutions, review them, then implement them.

The continued effort by the groups had a significant impact on the rest of the staff. Division staff members were surprised that the groups were still operating and still receiving executive support. Staff members not involved in the groups began to experiment with working more independently, questioning decisions seemingly made solely to conform to political requirements. Managers began to ask their staff to provide more input, explaining the business logic of their ideas and actions. The new behavior was immediately reinforced when the executives supported the new behavior in a memorandum summarizing the "off-site" experience.

The grapevine was swamped with interpretations of the new direction and philosophy. The reaction was typically one of surprise and doubt, particularly in offices that were most dependent on executive decisions. The executives had anticipated the rumors and questioning process, asking that "off-site" participants share their experiences with peers and to correct any rumors that distorted or denied the positive efforts of the "off-site." Their intervention into the grapevine ameliorated the negative ground swell that followed any major executive change, and kept the grapevine from totally distorting the new mission and philosophy.

Tying It All Together

Attending the annual sales conference had been the division's traditional reward for a high performers. The three days were filled with executives presenting revised administrative processes, new sales incentives and programs, and high-priced motivational speakers who challenged participants to rise to their full potential. The real highlights of the old sales conferences were the cocktail parties, the banquets, and the after hours parties. Only sales staff were invited and only sales issues were discussed.

The executive team demonstrated their commitment to the new philosophy by taking a major risk in redesigning the conference. Representatives from the managers' groups recommended to the executives that they shift the focus of the sales conference from a party atmosphere to a working environment. Instead of hiring motivational speakers, the representatives suggested that the executives involve the sales staff and key administrative and technical staff in the organizational redesign process begun at the "off-site."

They recommended that the conference start by updating the participants and involve the them in a process shorter, but similar to the one the groups had been involved in at the "off-site." The participants then would attend presentations by the groups on the key issues and the proposed solutions. During the presentations, sales conference participants would be asked to provide criticism and input into the recommended solutions. Two of the three days of the conference were to be devoted to working on organizational redesign. The third day was to remain traditional, featuring executives from other divisions presenting their yearly summaries and sharing strategic direction.

The executives feared that the sales conference participants would object to the new format, refusing to participate actively in the organizational redesign process. They were also concerned that the sales staff would resent the administrative and technical staff attending and participating as equals. Despite their fears, the executives decided that the best way to support the mission and philosophy was to risk redesigning the conference and evaluating the results. If the conference failed, they would slow the pace of the change and reconsider the strategy of having the staff drive the change. They believed, however, that the pressing business imperatives necessitated the risk and outweighed the possible negative impact.

Results

The sales conference was an overwhelming success. The participants eagerly joined in the shortened "off-site" process, became fully involved in the group presentations, and were very receptive to the administrative and technical staff participating. They quickly endorsed the new mission and philosophy, understanding the strategic need and the business opportunities and challenges presented by the mission.

More significantly, they wholeheartedly supported the organizational redesign process. They felt the redesign process was the best sales support tool or program that the division executives could implement. In fact, they urged the managers' groups to drastically reduce sales-incentive programs and institute a straight-forward commission program that rewarded the top performers. Additionally, they supported the administrative and technical staff attending the conference. They felt that the best way to develop team work and reduce the bureaucratic processes was to involve the staff from different functions in the redesign process.

The success of the conference, with the sales staff wholeheartedly embracing the effort to move to a new way of working, taught the executives the power of identifying the new mission and philosophy. They were amazed how much the organization had changed in nine weeks and how quickly everyone embraced building a flexible organization. The executives had unleashed a philosophical concept that was so strong that it changed the organization, the team, and the individual tiers of the division.

Redesigning a Team's Work Processes

Overview

Most organizational change efforts do not start from the top down, as the telecommunications division did in the previous example. They begin wherever a leader can link a compelling purpose, such as a market shift or the threat of increased competition, to a process, a structure, or set of behaviors that need to be improved. "Redesigning a Team's Work Processes" exemplifies this more typical kind of change.

This example illustrates several key points in the process of organizational change. First, it demonstrates how changes in the team tier spread up to the organizational tier and down to the individual tier. Second, it shows how the change ripples laterally outward within a tier, altering the organizational components. Third, it highlights how change can spread throughout an organization when the genetic core choses not to lead or fully support needed change.

Background

The company, a furniture manufacturer, employed 1200 people at one location, in three connected facilities. During the 1970s the company grew rapidly, adding buildings, equipment, and people, as quickly as possible. The rapid growth outstripped management's ability to efficiently control the manufacturing process. Consequently, manufacturing lead times (how long it takes to make the product) grew, increasing from four weeks to sixteen to twenty. The sales force promised delivery dates that the manufacturing function could not meet, and on-time delivery rates plunged. Customer satisfaction fell, and competitors began to erode the company's market share.

By the early eighties, the company's infrastructure was in shambles. The executive team was fragmented. The CEO used a "divide and conquer" management style to play one function against the other, believing that he could trust no one. Each of his senior executives ruled their function with impunity and with no regard for the consequences of their behavior. The company succeeded in despite of itself because of a well-know, highly-regarded brand name. The company remained highly profitable, and the owners were content to allow the company to struggle in a state of immense incongruency.

A new manufacturing vice president, hired on the advice of a limited investor, initiated a change process designed to rebuild the company's infrastructure. The effort made some significant gains, greatly improving on-time delivery (the date the product was promised to be delivered), but failed to decrease lead times. Most of the change effort focused on increasing cross-functional coordination, decreasing deliberate attempts to undermine other functions, and building a company wide management information system. In short, the new manufacturing vice president's energy was focused on managing the politics of his direct subordinates and his peers.

The owner had rarely supported the manufacturing vice president's efforts, simply requiring that the bottom line continually improve. In fact, the owner was a significant cause of the fierce and nasty politics, regularly interfering in the politics to please someone he favored within the organization. Like his CEO, he amused himself by playing one executive against the other, bestowing favors one day and punishing the next. However, other business interests demanded that he raise large amounts of capital and he decided to sell the company. To improve the company's value and market attractiveness, he decided that the company needed to redesign its basic way of manufacturing.

He hired a well-known consulting firm to implement a Just-In-Time manufacturing process. Consistent with his usual pattern of behavior, he dismissed them before the process was completely implemented. The firm was able, however, to complete a redesign of the manufacturing function, streamlining and rationalizing the basic work processes of the shop floor teams. The impact of redesigning the team's work processes was enormous. The shop-floor teams, who had been historically ignored, overworked, and blamed for the lead time problems, suddenly flourished.

Building Teams by Redesigning Work Processes

Why was a redesign in work processes so significant? The physical changes and the work processes changes were new to the company, but not revolutionary. The consultants did not use any superior methodologies or approaches. In fact, most of the shop-floor workers disliked the consultants, frequently ridiculing them or even, on one occasion, threatening them. The company politics remained as awful as always. In fact, they became worse, as the vice president of manufacturing was fired and an old crony of the owner replaced him.

The teams flourished because the consultants recommended layouts and new work processes that were long overdue and that made intuitive sense to the workers. The consultants provided information that the workers needed and had no other way of obtaining. Additionally, the consultants' advice superseded the manufacturing engineering department's advice which was mainly designed to curry political favor with other departments. In short, the change on the work processes made the daily work of the shop-floor staff easier and more productive.

The shop-floor workers seized the opportunity to redesign the lay-out. They were delighted that the manufacturing process was divided into manageable cells, with a *kanban* system that allowed them to take the time to ensure quality, maintain productivity, and assist each other when they were back-logged. They were furious, however, that the system was imposed on them. They were even angrier that the managers and supervisors wanted to take credit for the productivity and quality gains. They correctly believed that the company was willing to make a major investment in the consultants and in new equipment, but refused to alter the vicious politics that skewered everyone, lowering the quality of work life. They were also very upset that the owner broke his promise of not reducing the health benefit package at the same time that he was investing in new equipment and consultants.

Managing Intentional Incongruency

Despite this environment—a nasty, highly-political, dehumanizing corporate culture—the teams thrived and the change to a less bureaucratic way of working spread. How the employees analyzed the situation explains why the change was successful and spread. Most of the company employees were very aware of the corporate culture and the company's well-known mismanagement. The informal organization was very strong and active. To counteract the company's mismanagement, the employees banded together. They supported each other by providing fairly accurate information about management intentions and politics, warning each other when to hide and when to stand up to each successive management issue.

Employees routinely performed the three-tier analysis because their job security depended on it. The company was located in a rural area and was the biggest employer in the area. Employees had to know exactly if and when they needed to look for another job because the job search would be long and hard. They survived because they knew how to avoid trouble, who to appease, and who they could trust. The only way to determine this was to understand how the current market dynamics and the company's strategy influenced the internal workings of the company.

Employees routinely performed the sophisticated analysis. They had correctly predicted that the company would make significant changes in the executive ranks when the owner and the marketing vice president decided to expand the product lines. Expanding product lines required that the company change from a craftsman-oriented manufacturing process to a production-shop process. The decision was indeed the trigger that prompted the hiring of the new manufacturing vice president. The employees further predicted that the information systems would have to be changed to match the requirement of a production shop, and that the MIS vice president would be fired despite his close ties to the owner and the Chief Financial Officer.

Consolidating Gains

By understanding the pattern of the genetic core and the dynamics of the company's marketplace, the employees were able to successfully predict the major trends in the organization. They understood that implementing a Just-In-Time manufacturing process would change their behavior and the behavior of employees in directly affected functions, but not that of the executives. They decided that the change was so desperately needed that they would support it and manage the incongruence. They realized that the organizational philosophy would never change as long the present owner remained in control. They understood, however, that their working philosophy must support Just-In-Time. They were willing to break the connection between organizational environment and their behavior to improve working conditions.

They did this by supporting and protecting the better executives. They supported those that engaged in little or no politics and encouraged those that supported the change and protected them from the politics. They were politically sensitive, understanding that some requirements from the owner and the key politically-anointed executives would have to be tolerated and managed. They responded to the political requests on a timely basis, providing no reason for the owner to interfere or stop the process. In essence, they adopted the company philosophy of political fiefdoms at the level above them, while at their level they eliminated unnecessary bureaucratic steps and political games.

At the team and individual level, they began applying peer pressure to influence key workers to change. Workers openly discussed how they felt each other performed, encouraging their peers to learn new skills, to take the risk of changing, and to help their colleagues by supporting the change. They were actively involved in redesigning the pay system, encouraging management to pay more for multiple skills. They recognized the value of teamwork, including facilitation and leadership skills in the multiple skill set required for team members. They shifted the focus of the employees from seniority to knowledge and performance, understanding that the long-term health of the company was a paramount issue for everyone.

New information flows and the *kanban* system provided them with new tools to understand the manufacturing process better. They learned to make strategic shop-floor decisions, instead of the traditional shrug of the shoulders and avoidance of decision making. They began to realize that learning the new way to manufacture was a type of job security in itself. They discovered that they were now more marketable when several employees were hired into better jobs in other companies because they understood how to work in a Just-In-Time environment.

Consequently, their personal philosophies and self images began to change. As they changed how they worked, they changed their personal philosophies, their behavior, and their sense of self-worth. When this happened, the changes on the shop floor had spread to the individual level and to the organizational level, all as predicted by the employees on the shop floor.

Building Around the Skills and Abilities of a Team Member

Overview

Creating a flexible organization is also possible by changing an individual's role and behavior and allowing the impact of that change to work its way up the tiers. Taking advantage of a person's natural skills can have a significant impact on individuals, teams, and the organization, even when that person is a hourly worker in a non-critical department. Organizational change does not have to be championed only by managers or executives. Sometimes, a major change in an individual can ripple outward and upward, changing the teams and the organization.

The three-tiered, interactive process is crucial in creating the change. At the individual level, a component is modified, creating change in the other individual components, and the entire individual changes his view of who he is and what he can do. His belief in himself and his changed behavior influence and impact the team components, which in turn, influence the organizational components.

Background

A typical example of this is Beverly Tiref (not her real name), an African-American central supply room worker in a 250-bed inner city community hospital. The hospital was one division of a hospital corporation in a mostly suburban region, in the mid 1980's, just before managed care. The hospital administration was struggling with an external market that featured:

1. the introduction of predetermined reimbursement rates;
2. a declining inner city population;
3. intense competition from two other inner-city hospitals;
4. heavy overhead, nursing and technical workers shortages; and
5. doctors who did not want to practice in the inner city.

Internally, the hospital was rigidly stratified by the usual health care class system of educational level, discipline, and good old boy networks. Turf wars between departments were common, long-standing, and frequently bitter. Less powerful department heads, such as physical therapy, central supply room, and transportation, went out of their way to avoid being seen by the more powerful department heads, such as nursing and anesthesiology. They automatically avoided anyone from the medical department.

Power games between departments were rampant. The medical staff would complain about the nursing staff, insisting that nurses needed to simply obey medical orders and policy, not question why the doctors had ordered a procedure. Nursing would comply by assigning the most inexperienced but non-questioning nurses to the complaining doctors, sending an unmistakable message of "watch what you ask for."

The power game then would trickle down the organization. Nursing would demand that central supply change the way that the second floor linen inventory was maintained. While complying with the demand, central supply would meet the requirements with the oldest and most difficult to work with sheets in the hospital. The message to the nurse manager was clear: do not think that you can command us as the doctors command you. As these games raged throughout the organization, one party or the other would lure administration into taking sides, hoping to gain at least a temporary advantage over another department.

These types of internal politics were the norm in healthcare. In fact, they were mild compared to the big medical and university hospitals which also had the politics of the university to add to the healthcare politics. Despite the norms of the industry, the hospital vice president believed that the only way to survive in an increasingly regulated and competitive market was to make his hospital a paragon of efficient teamwork. Consequently, he took advantage of a corporate sponsored "patient-centered program" to break down the barriers between the various departments. He and his executive team used the "patient-centered program" as a theme to improve intra-hospital coordination and teamwork.

A Tiny and Important Center of Excellence

Most of the hospital employees were skeptical about the program making a difference. Most had seen administrators come and go, programs enthusiastically supported for a month or two, then dropped. All the while, politics remained at the usual levels. Beverly Tiref was one of the skeptics, a strong, vocal skeptic within her own area. She had been employed at the hospital for twenty years, working in several jobs, from unit clerk to operating room orderly. She was bright, competent, and under employed, a fact that she was well aware of. Nonetheless, she had learned that was the best way she could survive in a political environment dominated by white, suburban males.

She was now the supervisor in charge of sterilizing the operating room instruments in the autoclave room. Three workers reported to her and she in turn reported to the Central Supply Room manager. The Central Supply Room (CSR) was a twenty-four hour, seven-day a week operation, that only received attention when something was not right. Symbolically, CSR was physically located in the very back of the hospital facility, in the oldest and most shabby corner of the building. It was so removed, that many employees, although they knew it existed, did not know where it was located.

Beverly was excellent at ensuring the instruments were properly sterilized. She had worked in the operating room for several years as an orderly, working closely with the surgeons and OR nurses, understanding the need for absolute sterility. She had enjoyed working in the OR, but had complained, one time too many, about how the OR Director's lack of management skills hurt patients and was banished to CSR.

Under her supervisor, she cleaned and sterilized instruments for several years. When the supervisor left, she was promoted to the sterilization area. She was warned when she was promoted that she was not in favor politically, that management was leery of her attitude, and that she should be very careful of what she said and who she said it to. She understood, having long ago accepted that as a fact of life. She was a high-school educated, African-American woman in a white organization where education and role were the status symbols. She understood, but did not accept, that she was not allowed to have an opinion or an observation that would help the hospital.

However, her pride in her own abilities and work demanded that she make the sterilization process the best that she could. She taught her workers the exact purpose of each instrument, the order that it was used in, and the operations it was used in. After the initial cleansing, she would have the workers hold each instrument, gain a feel for how to use it, and understand its critical importance. She insisted that every worker be able to do all the jobs in the sterilization room, so that all were interchangeable, able to fill in for each other in an emergency. She taught them how to speed the process when the OR was backed up with emergencies and the demand for instruments was high. She taught them various sequences of wrapping the instruments, noting how each doctor preferred the sequence, and making special packages for each.

Her workers inspected each instrument, noting unusual wear and tear, and recommending replacement when necessary. Beverly groomed her successor, teaching her how to listen to the needs of the doctors and nurses, and her co-workers. She taught her how to manage the CSR managers and how to get them to purchase equipment when it was needed. Above all, she taught her workers to have pride in themselves and their work, establishing an environment that radiated professionalism. Consequently, her managerial abilities often threatened the CSR managers who felt that she was overly proud and protective of her little, unimportant area.

But Beverly knew better than to become trapped in their jealously. She understood that instrument sterilization was a small area in a large pond and that she was unimportant. However, she also understood that sterilized instruments were one of many critical factors in operating a surgical suite. If her department failed to properly sterilize an instrument, a patient could die. She understood that although the work she and her workers did seemed unimportant, it was also on the critical path in successful surgical operations. Consequently, she ignored the jealousy of the CSR managers, stubbornly stuck to her principles, and created a tiny center of excellence.

Seizing the Opportunity for Change

Beverly resigned herself to staying in her tiny sphere of excellence, unappreciated and unknown by management. However, she was a leader in the informal African-American network in the hospital and a respected member of the overall informal network. She always knew what was going on throughout the hospital, frequently reaching out to fellow employees who needed support, counseling, or advice. She was known for her tough approach. She gave hard, realistic assessments of why people kept getting themselves into trouble, and tough advice on how to stay out of trouble.

Within the formal organization, she was known not only as the CSR worker who had bitterly complained about the lack of patient care in the OR, but seen as someone who was not afraid to state her opinions about the lack of patient care in other departments. She was viewed as a trouble maker who somehow made the sterilization room work well. She was clearly someone to be avoided and not bothered. Like the CSR location, she was out of sight and out of mind. No one wanted to tangle with Beverly and no one wanted to involve her in any process to improve the hospital. Her honesty and commitment to the patient made her dangerous. She refused to understand why it was impossible to provide a higher standard of care to patients. She had proved it was possible in her area and wondered why the well-educated, highly-paid professional managers could not do as she did.

She watched from a distance as the department heads struggled with each other in their efforts to begin work cross-functionally. She laughed as she watched them position themselves as superior to their peers, as more patient centered than the others. She grew angry when they denied their department's errors and problems, and furious when they blamed CSR for their mistakes. However, she continued her strategy of maintaining a low profile and avoiding the lime light. She was constantly concerned that she would get caught in political cross fire, and because of her status and reputation, lose her job.

She became inadvertently involved in the change process when she made an off-hand remark to a young manager passing in the halls. Her comment was very helpful in creating a process to improve cooperation between the CSR and the OR. The manager suggested the idea to the management team where it was well received. The manager began to visit Beverly's department to discuss ideas and ways to improve cross-functional cooperation. Beverly's common sense and natural interpersonal skills made a positive impression on the manager and the management team.

Leading and Creating Team Change

The CSR was still plagued with management problems. Performance was poor, employee morale was low, and quality was sporadic. After a particularly bad incident, the vice president fired the CSR manager and at the urging of the young manager, appointed Beverly as acting manager of the CSR. The vice president told her that he planned to hire a new CSR manager from outside the hospital, someone who had proven managerial experience in CSRs. Beverly, anticipating this response, had decided that she would accept the position anyway, and proceeded to take charge.

She first attacked the absenteeism that plagued the department, confronting the major offenders by telling them that she expected them at work on time everyday. She stressed that their contributions were important to the department and that she did not care what anyone else thought about CSR. She demanded that the employees understand the important role that CSR played in providing excellent patient care. As long as they understood their importance, no one else's opinion mattered.

After speaking with the chronic offenders first, she met with every employee in the department. She asked them what they needed from her to do their job better, what they needed from the hospital to do their job better, and what they needed to do better as individual contributors to the CSR. She began to track the CSR's performance by measuring inventory levels, replenishment cycle time, and reported errors. She came in to the CSR at off hours, meeting with the swing and night shift employees. She promoted two long-term workers, proven performers, to supervisors, and held them accountable for performance on their shifts.

When Beverly first attended the monthly department head meetings, she remained quiet and reserved. She was open to criticism about her department's performance, but refrained from discussing other department's performance or ways to improve coordination. She viewed herself as the junior person in the meetings, and as acting manager, not entitled to the respect and position of the other managers. She was well aware of executive management's opinion of her as a troublemaker. She felt that she needed to maintain a low profile so that she could continue to lead the CSR employees in making CSR an outstanding department.

Organizational Change

Executive management continued to search for a new CSR manager during the next nine months. However, they soon began to notice that CSR was performing better, that absenteeism was significantly reduced, and that the number of complaints were down. The vice president was leaning toward promoting Beverly to manager, when he heard that Beverly and a nursing unit manager had a heated discussion during the department head meeting. The nursing unit manager had complained to the director of nursing that CSR had not replenished key supplies in her units. Beverly contradicted her, saying that the real issue was nursing's refusal to keep track of supplies and fill out the required replenishment forms. The vice president quickly viewed this as Beverly defending her turf, blaming someone else for her department's error, and becoming part of the political problem.

He met with Beverly privately, shared his displeasure, and reprimanded her. To his surprise, Beverly simply told him that he was making a mistake, that the nursing unit manager had a long history of not doing her job well, blaming other departments to hide her incompetence. She added that she did not expect him to believe her nor did she expect other department heads to support her. Most of the department heads had clashed with the nursing unit manager before and had lost, and now were not eager to get into a political battle with her again.

The vice president responded that he was disappointed with such a heretical view, and that he had been hoping that she would rise above the politics of the hospital. Beverly told him that she had always been above the politics of the hospital, and that she was only interested in working toward what was best for the patient. She also repeated that she did not expect him to believe her.

The vice president was taken aback by the entire interaction and spoke with the young manager. The young manager, uncharacteristically, spoke up for Beverly and against the nursing unit manager, normally a major political error. The vice president again was amazed by the unusual behavior and decided to observe carefully both the CSR and the nursing unit manager. Over the next three months, the pattern that Beverly had pointed out was repeated over and over. As the vice president and his executive team observed closely, they saw that the nursing unit manager was a political terror. She continually abused her position and influence to cover up her unit's lack of cross-functional cooperation.

When the vice president and the director of nursing became clear on the real pattern of behavior, they removed the nursing unit manager. They also promoted Beverly to CSR manager, thanking her for her honesty and commitment to superior patient care. Eighteen months later, Beverly Tiref was honored as manager of the year at the annual corporate banquet.

The circumstances that provided Beverly with the opportunity to demonstrate her abilities to her team became a major influence on her team, her department, and eventually the hospital. A change in an individual's role within the team allowed her to demonstrate behavior that changed embedded work processes in the CSR team. Her philosophy and commitment to providing the best patient care possible also permeated her team and department. As her strengths interacted with the team's organizational components, everyone changed. And once the team solidified their change, the organization began to change. As the organization changed, the process began to flow downward, Beverly became more experienced and a stronger leader, her team became stronger, and she in turn became a stronger person.

Chapter Eight
Implications

"Civilizations, I believe, come to birth and proceed to grow by success
fully responding to successive challenges. They break down and go to
pieces if and when a challenge confronts them which they fail to meet."

Arnold Toynbee
Civilization on Trial

The late twentieth century marketplace is in transitional turmoil,
confusing and complex. The world markets are increasingly global, the
Information Age is blossoming, and the Knowledge Age looms ahead
(see Chapter 1). The rapid change forces organizations to reinvent themselves as each age evolves into the next. Global organizations must discover how to be extremely sophisticated to deal with the complexity of
hundreds of regional markets while responding to minute variations in
very local markets. Information Age organizations must develop the ability to gather, collect, process, and disseminate millions of bytes of disparate data in a way meaningful to the employees who need to use it on
a daily basis. The Knowledge Age will force organizations to once again
reinvent themselves. Companies will need to learn how to market, sell,
and service knowledge rather than information. They will need to learn
how to continually build new knowledge as a core competency.

Organizations will be continually evolving to meet these new challenges. Successful organizations in the coming years will be those that are
highly flexible, responding to the multiple and conflicting demands of the
market. Flexible organizations will develop new structures, new systems,
new ways of working to manage contradictions such as, managing glob-
ally while responding locally, and encouraging diversity while creating
corporate commonalties. Many of the solutions to these issues will evolve
within the organizations, as illustrated in Chapter 7.

The three cases in Chapter 7 highlight three major phenomena of
organizational change. Organizational change:

1. occurs both on a planned and an unplanned basis;
2. occurs at the individual, team, and organizational level as people see and strive to correct incongruencies in the organization; and
3. is a process driven by people.

In the midst of all the turmoil, executives who believe that they and their executive team control the organization are deluding themselves. Organizational change is an inevitable process. Whether the company is poorly led, as in the case of redesigning work team processes, or well led, as in the case of Beverly Tiref, individuals will change the organization to match their sense of what is best for them and the organization. Unless their efforts are deliberately blocked, the changes will spread throughout the organization by flowing up, down and through the organizational components and tiers. Their efforts are the natural rebalancing process of any living organism. In all organizations, this natural effort is done by people.

Executives must not assume that people are naturally well-informed and will know what is best for the organization without an understanding of the organization's strategy, purpose, and philosophy. Rather they need to understand that they must provide employees with the information and knowledge about the organization's needs. This information and knowledge will provide the employees with an understanding of the overlap between their needs and the organizations needs. When employees see and understand the overlap, the natural change process of meeting both individual and organizational needs occurs (as illustrated in chapter 6).

As executives provide this information, they will find that approximately one-third of the employees will frequently see the organization's needs as matching their own needs. Another third of the employees will do their best to try to meet the organization's needs because they believe that is what they should do. The final one third is composed of two groups, those that always see the organization as imperfect and needing to make major changes, and those that will never be content in the organization.[18]

---

[18] This observation is based on the author's consulting experience. The general breakout of how people respond to organizational leadership is also shared by many other management consultants the author has worked with. It is also reinforced by the literature on responses of hypnotic subjects.

If executives focus on creating an overlap between the organization's needs and the individual's needs, they will no longer see the role of management as the need to control people. They will readily understand that organizations need policy and procedures to guide people, not to control them. Executives that try to control people are directing their efforts to the one-sixth of the employees who are not pleased working in the organization and will not be influenced no matter what is done. Executives must remember that this group is tiny, and should not create control mechanisms for everyone which are aimed at just this one-sixth. Rather they should focus on managing the one-sixth as a special case and leading the others. By letting go of the need to control the one-sixth, executives free the others to create flexible, responsive organizations.

Executives can leverage the organizational change phenomena to speed the process of change and to increase organizational flexibility. To leverage these phenomena, executives must:

- ❑ view their companies as People-Centered Organizations®;
- ❑ understand that their companies are in a continual state of flux, as people rebalance the organizational components to match shifts in the market or strategies;
- ❑ encourage the natural tendency of people to change the organization;
- ❑ develop and communicate strategic frameworks to everyone in the company;
- ❑ view their role as one of leadership rather than control;
- ❑ develop a process to learn about the natural changes that are occurring within the company and nurture those that will benefit the organization; and
- ❑ encourage employees and managers to use the three-tiered analysis as a framework to guide organizational change.

When executives lead their organizations and act in the manner above, they will find that their perspective changes. They will see the organization in a different light that enables them to understand:

1. When an organization is not changing, when people are not trying to make adjustments, the organization has a major problem.

2. When people are not performing to expectations, the most likely problem is an organizational incongruency. Executives should seek to correct the incongruency, prior to trying to solve the problem as an individual problem. (see chapter 2).

3. Leading an organization is a process of continually realigning the organization's strategy to the market, and the organizational components to the strategy.

4. Change starts from within the organization, or the team, or the individual, and spreads out. Change may be motivated by inside or outside forces, *but lasting change always starts from within.*

BIBLIOGRAPHY

Adizes, I. *Corporate Lifecycles.* Prentice-Hall: Englewood Cliffs, New Jersey, 1988.

Andolfi, Maurizo, et. al. *Behind the Family Mask: Therapeutic Change in Rigid Family Systems.* New York: Brunner/Mazel, Publishers, 1983.

Argyris, Chris. *Overcoming Organizational Defenses: Facilitating Organizational Learning.* Allyn-Bacon, 1990.

Argyris, Chris. "Skilled Incompetence," *Harvard Business Review.* September-October, 1986, p. 74.

Barge, Bruce and Carlson, John G. *Controlling Health Care and Disability Costs,* New York: John Wiley and Sons, Inc., 1993, p. 198.

Bandler, Richard and Grinder, John. *Frogs Into Princes: Neuro Lingusitic Programming.* Moab, Utah: Real People Press, 1979.

Bartlett, Christopher A. and Ghoshal, Sumantra. "Matrix Management: Not a Structure, A Frame of Mind," *Harvard Business Review.* July-August, 1990, pp. 138-145.

Bechard, Richard and Harris, Robert. *Organizational Transitions.* Reading, MA.: Addison-Wesley, 1987.

Beer, Michael, Eisenstat, R. A., and Spector, Bert. "Why Change Programs Don't Produce Change," *Harvard Business Review.* November-December, 1990, pp. 158-166.

Belasco, James A. *Teaching the Elephant to Dance.* New York: Crown Publishers, Inc., 1990.

Bridges, William. *The Character of Organizations.* Palo Alto, CA: Consulting Psychologists Press, Inc., 1992.

Burns, Tom and Stalker, G. M. *The Management of Innovation.* Chicago, IL: Quadrangle Books, 1962.

Capra, Fritjof. *The Tao of Physics.* Boston: Shamboala Publications, 1991.

Chandler, Alfred, Jr. *Strategy and Structure:Chapters in the History of the American Industrial Enterprise.* Cambridge, MA: M.I.T. Press, 1962.

Constantine, Larry S. "Organizational Development and the Family Therapist," *Family Therapy News.* June, 1992, pp. 17-18.

Deal, T. E. and Kennedy, A. A. *Corporate Culture: The Rites and Rituals of Corporate Life.* Reading, MA.: Addison-Wesley, 1982.

135

Emery, F. E. *Systems Thinking.* Baltimore, Md.: Penguin Books, Inc., 1979.

Erickson, Milton H. *Creative Choice in Hypnosis: Volume IV, The Seminars, Workshops, and Lectures of Milton H. Erickson,* edited by Ernest L. Rossi and Margaret O. Ryan. New York: Irvington Publishers, Inc., 1992.

Evans, Paul A. L. "Management Development on QWE Technology," *Human Resource Planning,* 15, 1992, pp. 85-106.

Galbraith, Jay. *Designing Complex Organizations.* Reading, Mass.: Addison-Wesley Publishing Company, 1973.

Groddeck, George. *The Book Of The It.* New York: Vintage Books, 1949.

Haley, Jay. *Leaving Home: The Therapy of Disturbed Young People.* New York: McGraw-Hill Book Company, 1980.

Hamel, G. and Prahalad, C. K. "Strategic Intent," *Harvard Business Review.* May-June, 1989, pp. 63-76.

Hammer, Michael. "Redesigning Work: Don't Automate, Obliterate." *Harvard Business Review.* July-August, 1990, pp. 104-112.

Hayes, Robert H. and Jaikuman Ramchandran. "Manufacturing's Crisis: New Technologies, Obsolete Organizations," *Harvard Business Review.* September-October, 1988, pp. 77-85

Hirschhorn, Larry and Gilmore, Thomas. "The New Boundaries of the Boundaryless Company," *Harvard Business Review.* May-June, 1992, pp. 104-115.

Johanson, Donald C. and Shreeve, James. *Lucy's Child: The Discovery of a Human Ancestor.* New York: William Morrow and Company, Inc., 1989.

Kantor, Rosabeth Moss. "Managing the Human Side of Change," *Management Review.* April, 1985, pp. 52-56.

Kanter, Rosabeth Moss. "Transcending Business Boundaries: 12,000 World Managers View Change," *Harvard Business Review.* May-June, 1991, pp. 151-164.

Kaptchuk, Ted J. *The Web That Has No Weaver.* New York: Congdon and Weed, Inc., 1983.

Lankton, Carol H. and Lankton, Stephen R. *Tales of Enchantment: Goal-Oriented Metaphors for Adults and Children in Therapy.* New York: Brunner/Mazel, Inc., 1989.

Lawler, Edward W. *High Involvement Organizations.* San Francisco: Jossey-Bass Inc., 1986.

Lawrence, Paul R. and Lorsch, Jay W. *Organization and Environment.* Boston, MA: Harvard Business School, Division of Research, 1967.

Leakey, Richard. *The Origin of Humankind.* New York: Basic Books, 1994.

Lewin, Kurt. *Field Theory in Social Science.* New York: Harper and Row Publishers, 1951.

Likert, Rensis. *The Human Organization.* New York: McGraw-Hill Book Company, 1967.

Lorsch, Jay W. and Morse, John J. *Organizations and Their Members: A Contingency Approach.* New York: Harper and Row Publishers, 1974.

Martin, Joanne. *Cultures In Organizations: Three Perspectives.* New York: Oxford University Press, Inc., 1992.

Mayo, Elton. *The Human Problems of an Industrial Civilization.* Boston: Graduate School of Business Administration, Harvard University, 1946.

McGregor, Douglas. *The Human Side of Enterprise.* New York: McGraw-Hill Book Company, 1960.

Miller, James G. "Living Systems: The Organization," *Behavioral Science* 17, 1, January 1972.

Minuchin, Salvador. *Families and Family Therapy.* Cambridge, MA: Harvard University Press, 1974.

Mintzberg, Henry. *Power In and Around Organizations.* Englewood Cliffs, NJ: Prentice-Hall, Inc., 1983.

Nadler, David A. "Managing Transitions to Uncertain Future States," *Organizational Dynamics.* Summer, 1982.

Niehaus, Richard J. and Price, Karl F. *Human Resource Strategies for Organizations In Transition.* New York: Plenium Press, 1989.

Palazzoli, Mara Selvini, et. al. *The Hidden Games of Organizations.* New York: Pantheon Books, 1986.

Palmer, Graham M. and Burns, Sherrill G. "Revolutionizing the Business: Strategies or Succeeding with Change," *Human Resources Planning,* 15, 1992, pp. 77-84.

Peters, Thomas J. and Waterman, Robert H. Jr. *In Search of Excellence.* New York: Harper and Row, Publishers, 1982.

Prahalad, C. K. and Hamel, G. "The Core Competence of the Corporation," *Harvard Business Review.* May-June, 1990, pp. 79-91.

O'Hanlon, Bill. "The Third Wave: The Promise of Narrative," *The Family Therapy Networker.* November-December, 1994, pp. 18-29.

Rank, Otto. *The Trauma of Birth.* London: Paul, Trench, Truber & Co., and Harcourt and Brace, 1929.

Rank, Otto. *Will Therapy and Truth and Reality,* translated by Jessie Taft. New York: Alfred Knopf, 1947.

Reimann, Bernard C. and Weiner, Yoash. "Corporate Culture: Avoiding the Elitist Trap," *Business Horizons.* March-April, 1988, pp. 36-44.

Rossi, Ernest L. *The Psychobiology of Mind-Body Healing: New Concepts of Therapeutic Hypnosis.* New York: W.W. Norton & Co, Inc., 1986.

Sashkin, Marshall and Kisser Ian. "What is TQM," *Executive Excellence.* May, 1992, p. 11.

Schaffer, Robert H. and Thomson, Harvey A. "Successful Change Programs Begin with Results," *Harvard Business Review.* January-February, 1992, pp. 80-89.

Sirken, Harold and Stalk, George, Jr. "Fix the Process, Not the Problem," Harvard *Business Review.* July-August, 1990, pp. 26-33.

Schein, Edgar H. *Organizational Culture and Leadership.* San Francisco, California: Jossey-Bass, Inc., 1985.

Sherwood, John J. "Creating Work Cultures with Competitive Advantage," *Organizational Dynamics.* Winter, 1988, pp. 5-27.

Taylor, Fredrick W. *The Principles of Scientific Management.* New York: W. W. Norton and Company, 1911.

Thompson, James D. *Organizations in Action.* New York: McGraw-Hill Book Company, 1967.

Walton, Richard W. "From Control to Commitment in the Workplace," *Harvard Business Review.* March-April, 1985, pp. 76-84.

Watzlawick, Paul, Weakland, John H., and Fisch, Richard. *Change: Principles of Problem Formation and Problem Resolution.* New York: W. W. Norton and Company, 1974.

Weber, Max. *Essays in Sociology,* edited by H. H. Gerth and C. Wright Mills. New York: Oxford University Press, 1974.

White, Alan F. "Organizational Transformation at BP: An Interview with Chairman and CEO Robert Horton," *Human Resource Planning,* 15, 1992, pp. 3-14.

Woodward, Jane. *Industrial Organization: Theory and Practice.* London: Oxford University Press, 1965.

Wynne, Lyman C., McDaniel, Susan H., and Weber, Timothy T. *Systems Consultation: A New Perspective for Family Therapy.* New York: The Guilford Press, 1986.

Zukav, Gary. *The Dancing Wu Li Masters: An Overview of the New Physics.* New York: William Morrow and Company, 1979